After the Apocalypse

After the Apocalypse

Srećko Horvat

polity

The right of Srećko Horvat to be identified as Author of this Work has been asserted in accordance with the UK Copyright, Designs and Patents Act 1988.

First published in 2021 by Polity Press
Reprinted 2021

Polity Press
65 Bridge Street
Cambridge CB2 1UR, UK

Polity Press
101 Station Landing
Suite 300
Medford, MA 02155, USA

The author wishes to thank KTH Centre for the Future of Places (CFP) and Director Dr. Tigran Haas for the research grant for the project.

THE CENTRE FOR THE
FUTURE OF PLACES

ISBN-13: 978-1-5095-4007-5
ISBN-13: 978-1-5095-4008-2 (pb)

A catalogue record for this book is available from the British Library.

Library of Congress Cataloging-in-Publication Data

Names: Horvat, Srećko, author.
Title: After the apocalypse / Srecko Horvat.
Description: Cambridge, UK ; Medford, MA : Polity, 2021. | Includes
  bibliographical references. | Summary: "A rollercoaster ride through the
  world after the Apocalypse with a simple message: either we change
  course or we face mass extinction"-- Provided by publisher.
Identifiers: LCCN 2020039921 (print) | LCCN 2020039922 (ebook) | ISBN
  9781509540075 | ISBN 9781509540082 (pb) | ISBN 9781509540099 (epub)
Subjects: LCSH: Civilization, Modern--21st century. | Regression
  (Civilization)
Classification: LCC D862.3 .H67 2021 (print) | LCC D862.3 (ebook) | DDC
  909.83/2--dc23
LC record available at https://lccn.loc.gov/2020039921
LC ebook record available at https://lccn.loc.gov/2020039922

Typeset in 11 on 13pt Sabon
by Fakenham Prepress Solutions, Fakenham, Norfolk NR21 8NL
Printed and bound in Great Britain by CPI Group (UK) Ltd, Croydon

The publisher has used its best endeavours to ensure that the URLs for external websites referred to in this book are correct and active at the time of going to press. However, the publisher has no responsibility for the websites and can make no guarantee that a site will remain live or that the content is or will remain appropriate.

Every effort has been made to trace all copyright holders, but if any have been overlooked the publisher will be pleased to include any necessary credits in any subsequent reprint or edition.

For further information on Polity, visit our website:
politybooks.com

Contents

Acknowledgements

To write a book about the Apocalypse even as it is in the process of unfolding makes an already difficult task even harder. We are all living through it, deeply entangled and personally shaken by its 'revelations', engulfed by its warnings and, yet, the attempt to imagine the unimaginable, to grasp the 'supraliminal', needs to be taken if we are to understand what is at stake, namely extinction. This book is not only an attempt to bridge these two tensions – overwhelming reality and the reality that is to come – it is, like every book, also a product of these times. I started to write it on the island of Vis, as a sort of continuation of my previous book *Poetry from the Future* (2019) and its chapter 'It's the End of the World (as We Know It)', and, after various travels to the 'future of places' (including Chernobyl), I sent the manuscript to my publisher in late January 2020. As I was awaiting feedback, I heard about a virus in China that would soon change the course of history not only as a dark 'real existing' dystopia, but also as a sort of rupture to open new – perhaps emancipatory – possibilities for a world 'after the Apocalypse'. In the meantime, I was stuck in Vienna during the COVID-19 lockdown until late May 2020 and received a message from my publisher John Thompson and two anonymous reviews of the first draft that easily convinced me, as hard as it was, to rewrite the whole book and to include the ongoing pandemic as an inherent part of the 'eschatological tipping points' that are being explored in this book. My deep gratitude goes to John, who published my first book written in English, *The Radicality of Love*, and who was immediately interested in publishing *After the Apocalypse*. Thanks to his never-ending patience, valuable comments and a few disagreements, the manuscript turned into its current form. I also want to thank the two anonymous reviewers who forced me to carefully rework some crucial parts of it; Sarah Dancy for the diligent copy-editing; and Julia Davies for her editorial support throughout the whole process.

This book started its life long before the current COVID-19 pandemic and the acceleration of catastrophes throughout the world, including climate crisis, civil wars and the enduring nuclear threat that are turning extinction not into a future event that is yet to come, but into something that might already become history once this book is published. If one day in March 2018 I hadn't met Tigran Haas in Stockholm, this book would perhaps never be written. I was invited by Tigran to deliver a lecture at the Center for the Future of Places at the KTH Royal Institute of Technology and immediately afterwards he told me I must write a book that would explore the 'future of places' in relation to the Apocalypse. Thanks to him and the generous support of the Center for the Future of Places, I decided to dive into this abyss and examine both the spatial and temporal implications of the Apocalypse. Only through numerous thoughts, dreams and fears shared with my fellow travellers, my *suputnik(s)* or *sputnik(s)*, did this book take its current shape. Perhaps a more precise term would be *supatnik* ('fellow sufferer'), as they had to endure my endless obsession with the 'end' and the 'after'. First and foremost, my thanks goes, as always, to Saša Savanović, not only for her critical comments and numerous readings, but also for making the world 'after the Apocalypse' a more joyful and hopeful place. Among my fellow travellers, whose list is long and always incomplete, those who especially helped in this endeavour are Franco 'Bifo' Berardi, Yanis Varoufakis, Darko Suvin, Boris Buden, Renata Ávila, Judith Meyer, Maja Kantar, Andrej Nikolaidis, Marko Pogačar, Valerio Baćak and Filip Balunović. This book was finished in the midst of a pandemic which, once again, proved that 'politics of friendship' is always connected to survival – and resistance.

Please note:
the post-apocalyptic fiction section has been moved to Current Affairs.*

* A sign in front of a bookstore in Massachusetts, November 2016, shortly after Donald Trump was elected President of the United States; sign at the window of a bookstore in Fowey, Cornwall, UK, January 2019, during the Brexit negotiations; sign in front of a bookstore in the fire-ravaged village of Cobargo, New South Wales, Australia, January 2020.

Introduction: Nine Theses on Apocalypse

> A fire broke out backstage in a theatre. The clown came
> out to warn the public; they thought it was a joke and
> applauded. He repeated it; the acclaim was even greater.
> I think that's just how the world will come to an end:
> to general applause from wits who believe it's a joke.
>
> Søren Kierkegaard, *Either/Or*, Part I, 1843

Empty streets and ghostly cities, curfew and quarantine;
closed shops, restaurants, schools and theatres; closed
borders between most countries in the world; around
three billion people in lockdown or in some sort
of isolation; thermal scanners, geolocation tracking
and mass surveillance; hundreds of millions of
workers unemployed; clear skies above us, a state
of exception beneath; hundreds of billions of locusts
swarming through parts of Africa and Asia, fuelled by
climate change; the biggest wildfires ever recorded in
the Chernobyl 'Exclusion Zone', coinciding with the
anniversary of the nuclear accident and an ongoing
pandemic; earthquakes and floods; authoritarian
capitalism and ecofascism on the rise across the world.

Before the year 2020, this would have sounded like a bad post-apocalyptic fiction movie that would probably get very poor reviews for an unconvincing script, or, as a friend of mine commented when, in March 2020, the Croatian capital Zagreb, already under lockdown due to the pandemic, was hit by the strongest earthquake in the last 140 years: 'If this was a movie at IMDb about a pandemic and then suddenly an earthquake happens, it wouldn't get even a 3/10 rating.' In other words, only a few months before 2020 officially started, this sort of scenario would have been regarded and dismissed as a bad joke by some version of Kierkegaard's clown.

Some people, influenced by the turning point presented by the 1917 October Revolution, were tempted to label the COVID-19 pandemic of spring 2020 'the hundred days that shook the world'. But what really happened in 2020 was not just a sudden and unexpected 'Apocalypse': it was a process that had been boiling beneath the surface of so-called 'normality' for decades. Whether the current situation will lead to a planetary revolution, or to a new form of destructive and authoritarian capitalism (or postcapitalism) and consequently to mass extinction, still remains uncertain. What is certain is that it was not just 'one hundred days' that shook the world: this was the result of a long process, of decades of neoliberalism and centuries of capitalism as the dominant world system based on extraction, exploitation and expansion, the effects of which suddenly surfaced in the year 2020 and, literally, infected our bodies and minds.

If some future historians, under the assumption that history will still exist after the demise of the human species, were to rediscover 'cave drawings' of contemporary humanity, what they would perhaps find among the ruins of late *Homo sapiens* would be a protective face mask, the true symbol of our contemporary times. Even if exact records about the surely mind-blowing number of face masks in circulation today could not be found, if future historians were lucky enough only to find newspaper 'remains' or social media data banks, they might well conclude that never before in the history of the world did so many people wear face masks as in the year 2020. All sorts of safety masks could have been seen in images already back in 2019, from all the continents of the world – from Belgrade and Santiago to Sydney and Hong Kong – whether they were used as protection against tear gas, severe air pollution or disastrous bushfires. Then, as if all this wasn't enough, a virus broke out in the midst of this already dystopian reality of impending climate crisis and authoritarian politics, and the face mask soon became the 'new normal' across the planet, an inevitable protective object of the late *Homo sapiens*.

When the first news of a highly contagious virus in Wuhan started to spread across the world in early January 2020, many believed – or wanted to believe – it was an epidemic that would not extend beyond China. But the virus had other intentions. As it was already, unbeknown to us, spreading across the world through the hyperconnected networks of global capitalism (its logistics and infrastructure: airlines, trains, cruisers, subways) and through the very sociability of humans (touches, hugs and kisses), we were following in real time how, just ahead of the Chinese New Year, the most important festivity in the country when hundreds of millions of Chinese temporarily migrate, the Chinese government imposed a travel ban and literally locked down 17 cities with almost 56 million people suddenly finding themselves in quarantine zones, prohibited from leaving them.[1] The epicentre of the coronavirus outbreak was the city of Wuhan, with a population of 11 million inhabitants. Suddenly, the streets of the so-called 'Chicago of China' were empty, like a ghost town. This was the future of places that would soon become the 'new normal' across the world. Yet, in early January 2020 it was as if the majority of the world's population was still living in a present that was already past, while China was already in the future.

In an attempt to stop the virus from spreading, the Chinese government prohibited any sort of transport inside the city of Wuhan as well as between other areas that had previously been connected to the Hubei region. Suddenly, there were no more flights, no cars or taxis; public transportation, including regional buses, was shut down and a ban on ships and ferries was imposed in other major cities. While the Chinese government delayed in letting the world know about coronavirus, the World Health Organization, instead of quickly warning the rest of the world and preparing them for something that was obviously not an epidemic confined just to China, but that presented a major global threat, described such a quarantine as 'unprecedented'.[2] However, even this unprecedented lockdown, which would in just a few weeks – in different forms – become the 'new normal' across the world, wasn't enough to contain the spread of the virus.

Even before it reached Europe and other parts of the world, it had already spread through the semiosphere (the realm of production and interpretation of signs) via social networks and history recordings made by 'smart phones' (often produced by a cheap labour force precisely in the sweatshops of China). From the seeming safety of our homes, we could have seen images of people fleeing Wuhan, and we were still watching it as a sort of post-apocalyptic movie that was not happening to us. Soon we would find out that, despite the lockdown, more than 5 million people had already left the city.[3] At the same time, local villages in the Hubei region took quarantine measures into their own hands: citizens self-organized and created 'protected bubbles' inside the contaminated areas by not letting in any strangers. Despite the fact that the Chinese government was trying hard to contain the spread of the virus, it was too late – the virus already started to fan out across the world. While some governments reacted quickly and contained the spread of the virus better than others, dangerous clowns in power – from Donald Trump to Boris Johnson and Jair Bolsonaro – were still thinking that the age of the pandemic was a joke, and instead applauded the new opportunities for disaster capitalism. Some governments, like that of Turkmenistan, even banned the word 'coronavirus', while others, like Viktor Orbán's government in Hungary, swiftly used the crisis in order to suspend parliamentary democracy and basically install a full-blown dictatorship within Europe. It seems that the virus appeared as a good 'excuse' to many regimes, which, instead of treating the virus as a serious health risk, used it to legitimize and finally fulfil their authoritarian wet dreams. As China was using its already dystopian surveillance system in order to trace infected bodies and manage their movements and behaviour, Silicon Valley companies were penetrating ever deeper into public infrastructure – for instance, through so-called 'smart cities' – and into crucial public services, such as healthcare systems around the world.[4] Those who were privileged enough not to be among the 'frontline' workers, but were confined to their homes, slowly woke up to a nightmare that was best captured by Naomi Klein, who called it the 'Screen New Deal'[5] – namely, a future where almost everything is 'shared' through the screen on a mediated platform. It is, as Klein points out, a future that employs fewer teachers, doctors and drivers, claiming to be running on 'artificial intelligence', but is 'actually held together by tens of millions of anonymous workers tucked away in warehouses, data centers, content moderation mills, electronic sweatshops, lithium mines, industrial farms, meat-processing plants, and prisons, where they are left unprotected from disease and hyperexploitation'.[6]

Even if this year – while I am writing these pages – still didn't come to its end, it can already be said that during 2020 world history accelerated to such a degree that we suddenly found ourselves in the future of an unprecedented planetary 'state of exception' and, at the same time, in a phase of imminent system crisis that would have effects not only on the future of humanity, but also on the future of the planet itself. Millions of flights were grounded, cruise lines suspended and cars parked for weeks, pushing the oil price below zero for the first time in history and leading to full oil tankers anchored with nowhere to unload. For a short moment, it looked like another world could still be possible. But before long, hundreds of millions of workers were left without an income, without a future, while it was precisely those very same big polluters – the car industry, airlines and oil companies – that were bailed out.[7] Everything had to change, so that everything could stay the same. Or even worse.

Even if, for a short dream-like moment, the skies above our cities were finally clear again, climate crisis continued to accelerate and deepen regardless of the perception that time had 'slowed down'. If 2019 was the year of global protest, from Fridays for Future to Extinction Rebellion, the massive and determined climate movement that was spreading across the world, then early 2020 was, to paraphrase the title of a good old science fiction movie, the year when 'the Earth stood still'.[8] Instead of the year of public protest, it was the year of quarantine. Instead of being on the streets, suddenly the majority of the world's population was confined to their homes. If you were lucky enough to have something called 'home'. This would, of course, change very soon. As the pandemic continued to rage in many corners of the world, when faced with new austerity, authoritarianism and structural racism, people took to the streets again, from Los Angeles to Sao Paolo, Minneapolis to London, to protest decades of austerity, rising authoritarianism, racism and structural violence. They were united by the words 'I can't breathe', protesting the suffocation caused by the structural violence of global capitalism.

Just before the global lockdown of early 2020, at a time when the post-apocalyptic fiction section had already been moved to current affairs, I was returning to a place I call 'home'. It is a remote island in the midst of the Adriatic Sea, where the first chapter of this book, 'Climate Crisis: Back to the Future Mediterranean', is taking place. It leads us to a reflection on the effects of climate crisis in a place that has not yet experienced the disastrous changes that so many other places in the world are already coping with: powerful hurricanes, rapidly rising sea levels and devastating droughts. But what if the year 2019 were a glance into the future of places where this would become the 'new normal' – even in the seemingly peaceful region of the Mediterranean? What if the hottest summers on record, stronger storms and recurring floods have to be understood as a warning – or rather 'revelation' – of the summers, winds and floods to come? The central concepts that are explored in this chapter on the changing Mediterranean are climate grief and 'solastalgia', but also, more broadly, 'post-apocalyptic melancholy' and the 'normalization' of the Apocalypse.

In the second chapter 'The Nuclear Age: 'Enjoy Chernobyl, Die Later' – the result of a trip to the so-called 'Exclusion Zone' just a few months before global air traffic and global tourism would literally be stopped – we move from the seemingly peaceful Mediterranean to somewhere that is already located 'after the Apocalypse', both as a place, and in time. What we encounter in this ghostly place of the future is not just the 'normalization' of disaster, but something that could be called the 'commodification' of the Apocalypse. This process of turning the Apocalypse into a consumerist product or experience takes various forms today, from cinema (the popular HBO *Chernobyl* series) and 'post-apocalyptic tourism' (not just to Chernobyl) to a wide range of products that reflect or materialize our current post-apocalyptic *Zeitgeist*. Besides looking at Chernobyl as an example of the 'commodification' of the Apocalypse, this chapter reminds us of the looming danger of nuclear catastrophe and introduces the thesis on the 'supraliminal' character of the nuclear age.

The third chapter, 'The Collision: Marshall Islands are Everywhere', starts with a speculative trip to the Marshall Islands, the most nuked place in the world as well as threatened by rapidly rising sea levels, in order to understand what happens when climate crisis and the nuclear age collide. What kind of consequences are there, not only on the future of places but on time itself? How do we transmit a message about nuclear waste, these 'pyramids of the twenty-first century', into the distant and uncertain future? Here, the term 'eschatological tipping points' is introduced in order to warn of the interconnectivity of eschatological threats that are not only all present at the same time, but are reaching 'tipping points' leading to an irreversible change in the Earth system. This is the final chapter in which the cover image of this book will be 'unveiled', something the Marshallese simply call the 'Tomb', but which could as well be the perfect illustration of what it means to be living 'after the Apocalypse'.

From the midst of the Pacific Ocean we come back to the year 2020 when, along with the nuclear age and climate crisis, the eschatological threat of a pandemic materialized and became 'normalized'. The coronavirus crisis hasn't ushered in the end of the world yet; it has been, rather, a 'revelation' in the original sense of the word 'Apocalypse'. A sort of an apocalyptic X-ray that has unveiled not only what the scientists were persistently warning of for decades (the destruction of wildlife and habitat loss creates the perfect conditions for spill-over of viruses from animals to humans). It also unmasked a global system based on a vicious circle of extraction, exploitation and expansion, which is leading not just to the 'ends of the world', but to an end of the ends of the world. The 'revelation' of COVID-19 is the following: the alternative is no longer socialism or barbarism, our only horizon today is a profound reinvention of the world or ... extinction.

What follows, before we begin on the journey into the world 'after the Apocalypse', are the main theses that will be further elaborated and recurring in the chapters of the book.

The Apocalypse already happened

Thesis 1: Extinction already happened if we continue with the current barbarism. We are living in the 'naked Apocalypse' without a kingdom to come.

'How can I save you? It already happened!' says James Cole (Bruce Willis) in the movie *12 Monkeys*, when a psychiatrist in a mental institution in 1990 asks him: 'Are you going to save us?' He's been considered crazy for claiming to be coming from the year 2035, a future in which almost the entire population of the world was annihilated by a deadly virus. To think of our present period as the time 'after the Apocalypse' requires, first and foremost, a similar shift in temporality. Not only did the Apocalypse as 'revelation' (see thesis 2) already happen, it is the end itself – the destruction of the biosphere and mass extinction – that happened in the future if we are unable to understand the 'revelation' of the rapidly unfolding planetary events and if we are not capable of radically reinventing the world in the time that remains. In order to come closer to an understanding of our contemporary 'revelation', we have to embark on a post-apocalyptic journey that follows an understanding of time that is opposite to the still prevailing conception of time as *chronos*. Namely, the idea – or rather ideology – of time as something 'linear', based on clocks, calendars and time zones, for centuries grounded in the capitalist notion of 'progress' and its myth that humanity is 'progressing' in a chronological order towards something meaningful, towards a 'higher' stage of civilization.

When we speak about 'progress' and Apocalypse, we should never forget that, as Déborah Danowski and Eduardo Viveiros de Castro warned us in their timely book *The Ends of The World* (2016), the end(s) of the world already happened – for someone, somewhere, and usually for those who were less privileged to benefit from what is usually called 'progress' (gunpowder, paper, religion, colonialism, capitalism).[9] However, the difference between our epoch and all the previous ones is that we are not just confronted with the 'ends of the world' that are simultaneously always happening. We are, and this is what makes our epoch the truly last epoch, faced with a possibility of an end that might end all other possible 'ends of the world', including epochality as such. What if there is nothing coming after the 'End-Time' – no new epoch, no new start, no promised kingdom?

Unlike the rather optimistic thesis of the 'kingdom without Apocalypse', present both in Judaeo-Christian eschatology and in the secularized versions of revolutionary movements, the seemingly counterintuitive thesis that the 'Apocalypse already happened' is closest to the philosophy of Günther Anders, an important but still overlooked philosopher of the twentieth century who spoke about a 'naked Apocalypse'.[10] According to Anders, it is 'naked' because there is nothing but a mere downfall awaiting us. There is no kingdom to come, only an 'Apocalypse without kingdom', which is in opposition both to Ezekielian eschatology and the capitalist faith in 'progress'. Or as Anders, whose thoughts and writings on the Apocalypse will crop up throughout this book, put it:

> Today, the fact that we have to live under the threat of a self-made apocalypse raises the moral problem in an entirely new way. Our moral task does not arise from the cancellation of the expected kingdom, from God's judgement, or from Christ (as Daniel and all other apocalypticians had expected). Our moral task arises because we ourselves, through our own doing, are responsible (not as judges, but nonetheless) for deciding whether our world will remain or disappear. We are the first to expect not the kingdom of God after the end, but nothing at all.[11]

Today, the end of the 'ends of the world' – not just the continuous and simultaneous ending of different worlds, but mass extinction and the destruction of the biosphere and the semiosphere – is even more likely than in the times when Anders was writing this passage. The catastrophe is not just simply in front of us: if we continue as if there were still a 'kingdom' to be reached after the Apocalypse, then the end has already happened, just like in *12 Monkeys*. The contours of this Apocalypse without a 'happy end', a revelation without the promise of an eternal kingdom of God, are explored in Chapter 2, 'The Nuclear Age: 'Enjoy Chernobyl, Die Later', and Chapter 3 'The Collision: Marshall Islands Are Everywhere'. If the Apocalypse already happened and there is no new beginning, no new epoch after this already dystopian epoch, then what we are living now is already the post-apocalyptic present in which our only horizon is the 'naked Apocalypse' – or *extinction*.

Apocalypse as revelation

Thesis 2: The Apocalypse is an X-ray machine from the future. What it enables is an unveiling of the architecture of our world, both as place and time.

The submicroscopic particle called SARS-CoV-2 that spread around the world in 2020 served in a way as a sort of an apocalyptic X-ray machine that exposed all the fallacies of our current world system based on expansion and extraction – from the short-term interests of governments and short-sighted 'market first' approaches to the profound underlying inequalities between and within our societies, between races and classes, between humans and other species. The COVID-19 pandemic was not the end of the world, but perhaps more than ever, since it was so imminent and visible in all spheres of life all across the world, we were reminded of the original meaning of the word 'Apocalypse'.

Although today, Apocalypse is commonly understood to mean 'the end of the world', the original Greek word *apokalypsis* (ἀποκάλυψις) reveals another reading. Coming from the Greek word roots of *apokalýp(tein)*, with *apo-* (meaning the prefix 'un-') and *kalyptein* (meaning 'to cover or conceal'), the 'apocalypse' was originally understood as 'uncovering' or 'unveiling'. The most famous apocalyptic text, the final book of the New Testament, was originally called Apocalypse, the title itself deriving from the first word of the text, written in Koine Greek *apokalypsis*, meaning 'revelation'. Originally, this referred to the 'revelation' of Jesus Christ, which was communicated to John of

Patmos. Despite the fact that the Book of Revelation is about both the end of the world and the resistance of early Christians, today's prevailing meaning of the term 'Apocalypse' as 'the final end of the world' originates from Modern English, when it started to denote the 'cataclysmic end of all things' (bringing it closer to the Greek meaning of *kataklysmos* as a 'deluge'), rather than the 'unveiling' (*apokalypsis*) of events to come. When the term 'Apocalypse' is used throughout this book, it is not referring to 'the end of the world', but to the 'unveiling' of the inevitability of the end of the world as we know it – namely, extinction.

What does it mean in practice for the Apocalypse to be understood as 'revelation' and not 'the end of the world'? When we encounter a catastrophe such as Hiroshima or Chernobyl, it can and must be interpreted not only as a man-made catastrophe that is an 'exception' to the rule, but rather as a 'revelation' about the nuclear age that introduces a set of new eschatological rules that didn't exist either in the prophetic visions of the biblical prophets or in human reality until the mid-twentieth century. And the same goes for the ongoing and deteriorating climate crisis that, according to scientists, even represents a new geological epoch, the so-called Anthropocene. From the perspective of the Apocalypse as 'revelation', the floods that hit the Mediterranean in 2019 were not a single random event, but an indication of the floods – and major climate disruptions – to come. The COVID-19 pandemic was a forerunner of the pandemics to come. And even if this sounds like an alarmist warning from Kierkegaard's clown, we should also note that the nuclear disasters of the twentieth century might become quite a small footnote to the planetary nuclear disaster to come – or, as a matter of fact, compared to the effects that the ongoing nuclear testings and the leaking nuclear waste are already having on humans, other species and the environment. All these disasters could have been avoided if we had listened to the scientists and if there were political will or, rather, an unprecedented transnational and intergenerational mobilization that would create the political subject capable of pulling the emergency brake. Perhaps, as Walter Benjamin famously warned in the fragment of his *One-Way Street* (1926) titled 'Fire Alarm', revolutions are an attempt by the passengers – namely, the human species – to activate the emergency brake on the train that is called 'progress'.

While in 2020 we had to 'flatten the curve' of the spread of a virus, in the years ahead – which are in fact already here – we must first and foremost 'flatten the curve' of climate crisis. But we must also, at the very same time, 'flatten the curve' of the impending nuclear threat – and it's not one or the other, but both, or rather all (eschatological threats) at the same time. If we just flatten the curve of the spread of a virus without a radical transformation of how we treat nature (extraction of resources, destruction of habitat, meat-consumption) and other human beings (inequality, racism, exploitation), nothing guarantees that another, even deadlier, virus won't appear next time, in ten years' time, or even sooner. In fact, it is becoming inevitable that everything, even the end of the world, might happen if we continue as if nothing had happened, as if 2020 were a short dream or temporary nightmare destined to fade out – or rather, be repressed – with the 'new normal'.

While the climate crisis is the most severe existential and eschatological threat, requiring immediate and determined collective action and a radical change in our understanding of 'progress' and 'growth', if we 'flatten the curve' of climate crisis without taking into consideration the nuclear threat, there is still a possibility that a nuclear war might lead to the end of the world, or an accidental leak to the extinction of the human species together with a wrecked biosphere. And in the same way, if we treat the pandemic just as a sudden intrusion into what was called 'normality' without questioning that very 'normality' (namely, the destruction of habitat and extinction of species that makes it inevitable that viruses jump from animals to humans), we won't be able to unmask and disable the 'new normality' (the further destruction of the planet) as something that is leading to an even bigger catastrophe (mass extinction).

And perhaps this is the most important warning to emerge from the COVID-19 pandemic: the Apocalypse (as 'revelation') doesn't have to come with a big bang, like an eruption of a super-volcano, destructive tsunami or rapid sea-level rise; it can come as an almost invisible particle, it can spread quickly and infect both the biological sphere and the semiosphere (see Thesis 3). It can happen anywhere, at any time, and in fact it is happening all the time. What the year 2020 unveiled is precisely the interconnectivity of simultaneous eschatological threats: countries across the world were hit by disastrous earthquakes, wildfires, locust invasions and floods at the same time as the pandemic. Even if, for a very brief moment, the skies were clear again and the oil stayed underground, the deteriorating climate crisis didn't stop, the nuclear threat didn't disappear and the threat of a much deadlier virus remains. Once these multiple eschatological threats meet and trigger a nonlinear change process, we can speak of 'eschatological tipping points' (Thesis 6) that are becoming more and more 'supraliminal' (Thesis 7).

The struggle for meaning

Thesis 3: The Apocalypse is always a semiotic machine. Disaster generates meaning. Meaning often generates disaster. Humans and the planet are so intertwined that it's no longer possible to make a clear separation between the biosphere and semiosphere.

It is the struggle for meaning that might as well determine the chances of our survival. If we understand the Apocalypse not as 'the end of the world', but as a revelation about the coming mass extinction, then the question is not only how we decipher the signs, but how we take control of meaning in order to respond to the 'revelation' about the end. Whenever humans, as a unique species generating meaning, encounter a past or future catastrophic event (not to mention the real possibility of the end of 'the ends of the world'), what is always already at play is *semiosis* – the process of signi-fication and production of meaning. In other words, the Apocalypse is never just simply a 'revelation' that takes place in the physical reality or the biosphere; it is at the same time a struggle for meaning in the semiosphere.

And again, we could have seen it in the year 2020 and in the ways COVID-19 was treated by various governments across the world, either as the 'Chinese virus', or as a 'hoax', or as another disease 'just like the flu', while scientists were persistently warning that the more we destroy habitats and continue with meat consumption, the more we will encounter pandemics – even more severe than COVID-19. The twenty-first century might as well be the century of pandemics. Yet, the coronavirus outbreak in 2020 wasn't just a virus that jumped from animals to humans; humans themselves made a mental jump as well. Once it infected the human species, language itself was affected. Once language was affected, human subjectivity was infected.

The new language ('flatten the curve', 'social distancing', 'self-isolation') created in 2020 as a result of the pandemic is a good illustration of how catastrophic events don't just affect the biosphere or infect biological bodies. The disaster takes place simultaneously in the semiosphere – the sphere of production and circulation of signs. Previous pandemics have also left their mark in language and human sociability. Why do we, for instance, still say 'bless you' when someone sneezes? According to some theories, expressions such as 'bless you', *'Gesundheit'* ('health') and *'nazdravlje'* ('to your health'), in numerous languages, are centuries old, and originated in the times when plague outbreaks were quite frequent, since sneezing was often the first sign that someone was infected. In other words, the language and social rules we are still using today are in fact the result of previous pandemics.

It was the French philosopher and psychotherapist Félix Guattari who, in his prophetic *The Three Ecologies* (published in French in 1989), already argued that we need to extend the definition of ecology to encompass not only the environmental sphere but also social relations and human subjectivity (a sort of 'mental ecology'). This ecosophical perspective (not to be mistaken with the philosophy of ecological equilibrium) not only takes into account the interconnections of the social/semiotic and environmental spheres; it also understands climate crisis as a direct result of the expansion of a new form of capitalism, a new world system that Guattari, back in the time when there were still two major political and ideological blocs and everyone was still speaking solely in terms of East–West or North–South relations, prophetically called 'integrated world capitalism':

> Contemporary capitalism can be defined as *integrated world capitalism*, because it tends toward a state where no human activity on the planet can escape it. It can be considered to have already colonized all the planet's surfaces, so that the essential aspect of its expression now concerns the new activities that it seeks to overcode and control.[12]

Instead of thinking nature as something separated from culture and the semiosphere, Guattari's ecosophical perspective questions the whole of subjectivity and capitalist power formations. This new world system, according to Guattari, 'not only intervenes in the world, it also penetrates us at the most personal level', namely at the unconscious level that also interacts 'with key components of the Integrated World Capitalism with an unprecedented and unexplored invasiveness'.[13]

The COVID-19 pandemic, as a consequence of a hyperintegrated world capitalism that destroys the biosphere through continuous extraction and expansion, has infected language itself. What better proof but words and concepts such as 'social distancing', 'self-isolation', 'return to normal', or even Angela Merkel's neologism *Öffnungsdiskussionsorgien* (meaning, para-phrased, 'orgies of discussion about reopening')? These new words that were provoked by the virus were not just mere words. They were a way of giving sense to a profoundly changing world and, at the same time, a way of constructing a redefined political, social and mental reality. As soon as we would take any of these concepts under the critical microscope, we would find in them not only a constructed relation to a disaster, but a narrative: for instance, how the phrases 'return to normal' or 'new normal' are actually part of a more complex process of the 'normalization' of the Apocalypse (see Thesis 5). As we will see in the third chapter of this book 'The Collision: Marshall Islands Are Everywhere', even such a seemingly carefree word as *bikini* hides the ideological struggle for meaning that was taking place in the background of a nuclear Apocalypse.

Catastrophic events always generate meaning and turn into narratives. It is thus impossible to think of the Apocalypse without being already submerged into the apocalyptic narrative that is as old as humanity, and with its mythologies constructed in order to cope with finitude, from the first cave paintings to the floods and dooms of the Bible and other religious texts. This, of course, doesn't mean that the current climate crisis or nuclear threat is merely a narrative – the current epoch represents something completely new in the history of human–Earth relations. At the same time, we should not forget that the current planetary crisis is affecting not only the biosphere but also the semiosphere, and thus human subjectivity, very often leading to a prevailing sense of fear, anxiety, depression, hopelessness and a specific sort of melancholy.

Post-apocalyptic melancholy

Thesis 4: The current devastation of the planet leaves deep scars not only on the surface of the Earth, but in human subjectivity. The overwhelming and prevailing sense of the end could be called the 'post-apocalyptic melancholy'.

The profound changes that we are experiencing on an everyday level, from the destruction of the environment to the age of pandemics, already transformed human subjectivity. The prevailing sensitivity that can be discerned today is a sort of 'post-apocalyptic melancholy', the sense of an ending that is unlike any other endings before, an ending that is inevitable if we continue with our current world system, an ending meaning the end of the biosphere and mass extinction, whether it is rapid or slow, the feeling that everything changes and that the only thing that's certain is extinction. This naturally creates anxiety – and leads to the difficulty, or rather impossibility, of coping with the irreversible loss.

This sort of 'post-apocalyptic melancholy' could have

been discerned in August 2019, at that time the hottest summer ever recorded, when Iceland held a funeral for its first glacier lost to climate crisis. As scientists warned that hundreds of other ice sheets on the subarctic island risk the same fate, a bronze plaque was mounted on a bare rock on the barren terrain once covered by the Okjökul glacier. The plaque reads:

A letter to the future
Ok is the first Icelandic glacier to lose its status as a glacier.
In the next two hundred years, all our glaciers are expected to follow the same path.
This monument is to acknowledge that we know what is happening and what needs to be done.
Only you know if we did it.
Ágúst 2019
415 ppm CO_2[14]

Only a month later, in what would become the hottest September ever recorded, another 'funeral march' took place. This time in the Swiss Alps, where activists (or rather mourners) marked the disappearance of the Pizol glacier, due to rising global temperatures. And, unfortunately, it seems that the funeral season has only just begun: a recent study by Swiss researchers suggests that by 2050, at least half of Switzerland's glaciers could vanish, while more than 90 per cent of glacier volume in the Alps could be lost by 2100.[15] This would mean, in order to visualize the scope of it, almost 4,000 funerals.[16] How do you mourn or ever overcome such a loss? As if this procession of funerals wasn't enough, in October 2019 thousands of activists from the environmental group Extinction Rebellion staged a symbolic 'funeral procession' for the planet in central London, carrying coffins and paper skeletons to draw attention to the ongoing climate crisis. One of the activists said:

'We're connecting with our grief for the huge amount of species that have already been lost, for those people who have already been impacted by climate change, for our brothers and sisters across the globe.'[17]

As funerals from Iceland and Switzerland to London were gaining ground just before the COVID-19 pandemic would make it impossible to enact similar public actions for at least the first several months of 2020, we could have seen a sort of grief not only for what has already been lost, but also for what will be lost. These funerals were not held just for the lost glaciers, they were funerals for all the glaciers that will be lost, and that are already lost if we continue to act as if this is only going to happen in a very distant future. It was a funeral for the planet destroyed by extraction and expansion. The contemporary 'climate grief' is thus closely related both to the disaster that already happened and to the disaster to come, including those that are in the process of happening. It makes our contemporary sensitivity rather complex: it is not just grief towards the loss, but also a sort of 'anticipatory grief' ('solastalgia') towards what will be lost or is in the process of being lost. This is explored further in the chapter: 'Climate Crisis: Back to the Future Mediterranean'.

However, 'grief' is perhaps not the best term to describe the actual feeling of the unprecedented loss that humanity is facing. When it is, at least according to Freud's famous text *Mourning and Melancholia*, impossible to come to terms with a loss that is too difficult to comprehend, what is at play is, rather, melancholia. While both mourning and melancholy derive from the loss, their outcomes are different. Mourning is a process through which we finally succeed in overcoming the suffering caused by an important and irreversible loss (for instance, the death of a beloved person). It doesn't mean that the loss disappears; it means, rather, that we can finally prevail over sorrow and learn to live with the loss. Melancholy, at least according to this theory, is a sort of 'unsuccessful' mourning, Freud even called it 'pathological', the impossibility of overcoming sorrow leading to an inability to live without the loss or, instead, turning loss into a commodity or fetish. Both end up betraying the loss.

Instead of this interpretation of melancholy, in order to understand what 'post-apocalyptic melancholy' means, and thus perhaps become able to cope with ecological grief and solastalgia, we have to return to the great German philosopher Walter Benjamin, who didn't strictly distinguish between mourning and melancholy. In the book *Trauerspiel* (literally, 'Mourning Play'), his early study of theatre plays during the baroque period in the late sixteenth and early seventeenth centuries, Benjamin exposed the implicit eschatological structure of those works. It is 'mourning' (*Trauer*) that is recognized as the predominant mood inherent to this structure. But what is interesting, as many readers of Benjamin have pointed out already, is how he doesn't follow the traditional dichotomy between mourning and melancholy. What we have at play here is, rather, a conjunction of mourning and melancholy. Instead of 'pathologizing melancholy', Benjamin rehabilitated the subversive potential of melancholy, showing that it always contains the possibility of its own undermining. The way to confront the dire reality in early modernity was a sort of dialectics of melancholy that was able to play (*spiel*) with mourning (*Trauer*), turning mourning into a potential political tool and thus coping with the loss in a more constructive way. For Benjamin, *history will have been*, and it is 'this peculiar form of *futur antérieur* that', as Sami Khatib notes, 'provides the structural condition of possibility for both the retro-active redemption of missed chances for happiness in the past and the anticipating pulling of the 'emergency brake' of the catastrophically racing train of capitalist modernity.'[18]

Faced with the possibility that the world as a whole – its biosphere and semiosphere – might come to an end precisely as a result of this capitalist modernity, it seems useful to return to Benjamin's understanding of melancholy, which, with all its ambiguities, perhaps contains the means to find a way to discover and pull the 'emergency brake'. Both 'climate grief' and 'solastalgia' remain important fields of research into our contemporary psychosphere, and they should become part of primary education, organization and activism worldwide, but what must be acknowledged at the same time is the melancholy that can't be reduced to mourning and can't be cured by it. Why? Simply because *the history that will have been* is called extinction. And this is a loss that is not just the loss of a beloved person, the loss of habitat, or even the loss of whole species. It is all of this together, and more. This loss is so big (see Thesis 7 on the 'supraliminal') that it encompasses all other losses. It is not only all our human experiences, including cultures and languages, architecture, art and science, that will disappear, it is the entire biosphere and other living species; it is the future itself that is being lost. And how do you mourn a loss that is not merely a future loss, but loss of the future itself? Very often, the response is 'normalization' (see Thesis 5), a process that turns the loss into a fetish or commodity (this is, among other things, the topic of the chapter on Chernobyl).

What Benjamin reminds us of is the dialectical potential of melancholy that would be neither a 'pathological' response to loss nor a commodification of grief. When the term 'post-apocalyptic melancholy' is used in this book, it is not only to describe the current *Zeitgeist*, but also to remind us of Benjamin's dialectics of melancholy that contains the possibility of finding a way out of the vicious circle of betraying the loss. The end of the world (mass extinction) is not just any loss. Nor is the death of someone you love just any loss. It can be the loss of a whole world. But just as the loss of a beloved person represents the loss of a whole world (which can lead to mourning or melancholy), so the loss that the 'post-apocalyptic melancholy' refers to is a loss that is impossible to mourn, because it is too big ('supraliminal') and represents a loss that already happened in the future. Yet, as dark as this sounds, 'post-apocalyptic melancholy' doesn't necessarily have to lead to that paralyzing feeling that we can't change anything. It is precisely the conjunction of post-apocalyptic melancholy (the impossibility of coming to terms with the loss) *and* unprecedented political action that offers a way out of our contemporary deadlock.

What if the only way to avoid betraying the loss (present in both mourning and melancholy) lies in de-pathologizing melancholy? To de-pathologize means to acknowledge the impossibility of mourning 'the history that will have been' and, at the same time, it means coping with the loss in a way that is constructive, not involving the usual characteristics of self-absorption and recycling of grief, but rather a subversion (or *spiel*) that could present a cure through which post-apocalyptic melancholy could become useful. When our horizon becomes extinction and we are faced with such an unprecedented loss, we have a responsibility towards future generations to properly understand and minimize the already existing eschatological threats, to warn them of the 'pyramids of the twenty-first century', a necropolis of radioactivity or deadly viruses, but also to construct a different end of the world. This should not just be a moral dictum, but our political duty. And it is precisely this duty or ethics – and unprecedented collective action indivisible from loss – that can perhaps teach us how to live with 'post-apocalyptic melancholy'.

'Normalization' of the Apocalypse

Thesis 5: The current devastation of the world is enabled through the process of 'normalizing' contemporary barbarism. Instead of 'returning to the normal', we should treat the 'normal' as the true problem.

The Apocalypse is not just an eschatological event, in an epoch in which the human species became the 'masters of the Apocalypse'; it is a political event *par excellence*. Or to put it into the context of the COVID-19 pandemic – as much as we needed science and medicine, the decision on how to deal with this eschatological threat was first and foremost a political decision that had everything to do with the economy and the capitalist notion of 'progress'. This is why all the powers of the old world – from populist leaders and authoritarian governments to the military-industrial complex and surveillance capitalism – have entered into a holy alliance to 'normalize' both the Apocalypse and the post-apocalyptic melancholy that is spreading faster than any virus.

The following were just some among the thousands of similar headlines from virtually every corner of the world in late spring 2020: 'Wuhan is on a slow path back to normality after 76-day coronavirus lockdown'; 'Merkel moves ahead with gradual return to normality in Germany'; 'A partial return to normality, police prepare for protests in Berlin'; 'Ireland faces "crawl back to normality" after coronavirus lockdown'; 'Italy is traumatised and normality is still only a distant dream'; 'Cyprus takes first step to gradual return to normality'; 'Britain has weeks to go before normality returns'; 'Canadians should expect weeks or months before life return to normal'.

The year 2020 could perhaps be called the year of

'normalization', or, more precisely, the year in which the ideology of 'normality' was exposed and at the same time reimposed, with martial law when needed. While the governments and corporations of the world were keen to return to 'normality' (to save the economy and ensure further 'progress') or were already preparing for what they would quickly call the 'new normal' (mass surveillance, restriction of movement, authoritarian capitalism, further exploitation of labour and natural resources), billions of people in various ways affected by the COVID-19 pandemic were, besides struggling to survive in a deteriorating dystopian reality, learning a new language and new sociability in the age of pandemics. Physical distance, fear of the Other and permanent anxiety, to name just a few, soon became part of a new sociability that was anything but normal. The rapid speed with which the virus spread through the world was enabled by the very infrastructure and logistics of the current global system based on extraction and expansion. Contemporary global cities, designed for cars and the circulation of human labour, are also anything but 'normal' and are not good for health, especially if we are going to live with a pandemic. The same goes for the privatization of public healthcare systems: not only is it harmful for the whole of society to underfund and destroy this invaluable sector, our future survival actually depends on doing precisely the opposite.

What the COVID-19 crisis unveiled (at least to those who didn't see it before or weren't aware of it) is that our survival depends on all the millions of so-called 'essential workers', from medical workers and care workers to seasonal agricultural workers and delivery workers, who not only ensure that our societies remain healthy, but also work in health-threatening and underpaid conditions so that delicious asparagus or a much-wanted book might arrive at the table of those who were lucky enough to have the means (a home, a job, a computer and internet; savings, family, friends) for the luxury of 'self-isolation' or 'social distancing'. Is this something we should be calling 'normal'?

Or take another image that became the 'new normal' in spring 2020, just before the United States was to face the biggest protests and social unrest since 1968 after the brutal racist murder of George Floyd. In the country with the highest COVID-19 death toll in the world at that time, military jets were flying over cities of New York, Philadelphia, Washington, DC, Baltimore and Atlanta to 'salute frontline workers'. Each of the 'Blue Angels' and 'Thunderbirds', worth hundreds of millions of dollars and burning thousands of gallons of fuel, could have been invested into the healthcare system and support for millions of people to help them to overcome unemployment and enable them to sustain themselves. But the creation of a 'new normal' (the pilots saluting frontline workers) was literally more important than saving human lives. It was disaster politics that was covering up the real problem. And while the US government was sending military jets in order to 'salute the frontline workers', all across Europe a new form of sociability was invented – namely, clapping from balconies or doorsteps in solidarity with so-called 'essential workers'. But even this gesture of solidarity wasn't really a gesture of solidarity; it was the 'normalization' of social distancing from the very (sacrificial) workers who have been on the so-called 'frontline', not only during the pandemic but for decades and throughout history. Even the discourse about healthcare workers as 'heroes' was another attempt to present the pandemic as a sort of 'natural catastrophe' or 'war', instead of understanding it as a disaster that was exacerbated – or even created – by global capitalism. What the process of 'normalization'

covers up is precisely how contingent and contested –
and therefore *political* – each Apocalypse is.

If there ever was a destructive ideology of the
twenty-first century, then it is this mythology of the
'return to normal', simply because it would mean a
return to the vicious circle of never-ending expansion,
extraction and exploitation, which, in the first place,
lead to the multiple and simultaneous eschatological
threats that we are facing today (climate crisis, nuclear
age, pandemics). This sort of 'normal' – a system based
on the ideology and reality of 'progress' (expansion,
extraction and exploitation) – is the very cause of the
'tipping points' we are reaching today.

Eschatological tipping points

*Thesis 6: Today, more than ever before, we are
confronted not by just one eschatological threat, but
by multiple and simultaneous threats that can function
as 'tipping points' leading to an irreversible planetary
change.*

The term 'tipping point', widely adopted among climate
scientists today, usually refers to a nonlinear rapid
change in parts of the climate system, a rapid shift that
happens when a system fails to cope with increasing
change. The system irreversibly 'tips' from one state
to another. Since the term has been widely used
across multiple disciplines (chemistry, mathematics,
social sciences, climate science), a team of researchers
recently proposed a unifying definition, according to
which a 'tipping point' presents 'a threshold at which
small quantitative changes in the system trigger a
non-linear change process that is driven by system-
internal feedback mechanisms and inevitably leads to a

qualitatively different state of the system, which is often irreversible'.[19]

In other words, global warming, ocean heatwaves, sea-ice thinning, permafrost melting, frequent droughts, species extinction: all can lead to a planetary cascade of tipping points that would not only give rise to uninhabitable 'hothouse' climate conditions, but provoke a system change that will be irreversible. In November 2019, on the fortieth anniversary of the first world climate conference, 11,000 scientists from 153 countries were prompted to declare: 'We're reaching potentially irreversible climate tipping points – climate chain reactions that could cause significant disruptions to ecosystems, society, and economies.'[20]

Throughout its history, humanity has been faced with numerous large-scale disasters; it could even be said that the history of humanity is nothing but a history of catastrophes that humans succeeded in overcoming. However, previous crises did not contain 'tipping points' that were, on the one hand, created by humanity itself and, on the other, irreversible, leading to a new Earth system that is not only beyond human control but also beyond our imagination. Tipping points in the climate system, as scientists and the global climate movement have been persistently warning over past decades, are increasingly leading towards such an irreversible point of no return. There is no doubt that the climate crisis presents an eschatological threat as never before, a rupture that encompasses the future of the whole planet, its biosphere and even its geology. But what if the term 'tipping point' were to be applied in addition to a sort of eschatology that concerns not just climate chain reactions, but also other *eschata* that are fully interconnected and likely to exacerbate the current situation? This is certainly not to say that the climate crisis is just one more apocalyptic event that follows others that have come before, or that it is just another threat among a plethora of threats. The point is to understand the complexity and interconnectedness of multiple eschatological threats – climate crisis, nuclear age, pandemics – in order to minimize the chances of a planetary cascade of 'eschatological tipping points'.

And again, the year 2020 didn't lack examples of such 'eschatological tipping points'. Even as the COVID-19 pandemic affected the lives of billions and infected the popular imagination of the majority of the world's population like no single event before, what was taking place during that turning point in human history wasn't just the spread of the virus. It is never just a virus. It is many threats combined at the same time, processes that are interconnected and that are increasing the severity of the unprecedented challenge faced by humanity. Multiple eschatological threats coexist as possibilities, or even as alternate realities: on the one hand, they are fully contingent (an asteroid hitting Earth is completely out of human control), while, on the other, they depend on us, as the only species that succeeded in coming to a level of evolution that implies not just an unprecedented ability of self-destruction, but also the capacity to destroy the biosphere and lead other species to extinction as well.

So if, on the one hand, we have eschatological threats that are fully out of human control (like asteroids, solar storms and super-volcanos), what threats such as the climate crisis, nuclear war and the age of the pandemic unveil are unprecedented hazards generated by humans and thus, perhaps, still sufficiently under human control – until we reach the eschatological 'tipping point'. This book deals with the threshold we are reaching with the latter, namely the eschatological threats that are possibly still under our control – but are becoming increasingly 'supraliminal'.

Extinction is 'supraliminal'

Thesis 7: The human species is capable of destroying the biosphere and at the same time unable to fully comprehend or anticipate all the repercussions of this capability. Extinction is supraliminal because it goes beyond the limits of our understanding, and even our imagination.

With the invention of the nuclear bomb, humans beings have become the 'masters of the Apocalypse'. According to Günther Anders, at that precise moment – symbolized by Hiroshima – the history of all past epochs was reduced to 'mere prehistory'. In the first epoch, all people were mortal. In the second, all people were 'killable'. In the third age, not only are people mortal or 'killable'; all humanity is 'killable'. We have now reached the fourth epoch, because the critical question is no longer about whether humanity will continue to exist or not, but whether the biosphere – and all living beings – will exist at all. With the collision of the nuclear age and climate crisis, we are reaching a stage of human history when the intensity and magnitude of this threat are becoming too big for us to fully comprehend.

Today, when pandemics and major climate disruptions have become the 'new normal', it is obvious more than ever before: if we continue with current levels of extraction and expansion, the only possible outcome is extinction. And it will entail the extinction of not only the human race, but all other species too. It will, at the same time, be the destruction of the biosphere and the annihilation of the semiosphere, as there will be no one left to give any meaning to the world after the end – no witness, no meaning. The COVID-19 pandemic has been a frightening glimpse (or an Apocalypse in the sense of *apokalýptein*) into the 'supraliminal' magnitude of eschatalogical threats that are no longer limited to the possibility of complete climate breakdown or nuclear war. Add a deadly virus to this already explosive eschatological mix, not to mention the eruption of a super-volcano, and we are faced with an eschatology that is beyond our ability to comprehend or even imagine.

In order to describe this total inability to deal with such an intensity, back in 1956, in the first volume of his book *Die Antiquiertheit des Menschen* (unfortunately still not translated into English), Anders coined the term 'supraliminal' (*überschwellig*). Writing about the nuclear age, he states that its consequences are 'supraliminal' in the sense that they exceed the limits of our understanding.[21] In contrast to the 'subliminal', which refers to the sensory stimuli that are below the threshold of conscious perception, the 'supraliminal' goes beyond that limit; it is literally too big to grasp. And it goes beyond that limit because no human can fully cope with the glimpse into a future without history.

Nuclear war or climate catastrophe – or both together – wouldn't be an historic disaster; it wouldn't take place *in* history, it would, rather, be the catastrophe *of* history, the true end of history. The very end of the world would become historically 'supraliminal'. The current eschatological tipping points are 'supraliminal' in the sense that they go not only beyond the threshold of what humans can comprehend, they literally go beyond history. Even if the planet were to continue to exist, there would be no more history.

Time beyond 'progress'

Thesis 8: We need an eschatology that will navigate us beyond the reductionist linear notion of time embodied in the capitalist understanding of 'progress'. Another end of the world is still possible if we are able to reinvent our understanding of time.

In January 2020, the 'Doomsday Clock' of the Bulletin of the Atomic Scientists was for the first time set at 100 seconds to midnight, or, as the scientists put it, it has been set 'closer to Apocalypse than ever'.[22] In their explanation of this decision, they stated that 'humanity continues to face two simultaneous existential dangers – nuclear war and climate change – that are compounded by a threat multiplier, cyber-enabled information warfare, that undercuts society's ability to respond'.[23]

The Doomsday Clock was set at 100 seconds to midnight when the virus was still thought to be only in Wuhan, just before we faced a pandemic that would further destabilize an already destabilized world order. At the same time as when the 'Earth stood still', history accelerated. Everything was simultaneously both slow and rapid. In a matter of weeks, hundreds of millions of workers became unemployed, billions of people were living under conditions of movement restrictions and/ or in some sort of isolation or quarantine. There was an unprecedented planetary 'state of exception' that affected not only human societies and economies, but the planet itself. Suddenly, we could hear the birds again and see wild animals in the cities; for once, we could even hear the planet and its seismic activity better than ever before – quite literally, because coronavirus 'quieted' the world.[24] But at the same time, the semiosphere was overloaded by information warfare, the world was full of fake news and many countries were governed by irresponsible leaders, which was, literally, resulting in more deaths – it is enough to remember Boris Johnson, who himself ended up in hospital infected by COVID-19, after downplaying the health risk the contagion represents, or Donald Trump who went so far as to suggest that 'injecting disinfectants' could be used to treat the virus.

As barbarism today accelerates to the degree that the whole planet is at stake, we must remember the warning of Günther Anders: 'We can be certain that we must run faster than people did in earlier times, even faster than the course of time itself; so that we overtake the course of time and secure its place in tomorrow before time itself arrives at tomorrow.'[25] In other words, our Herculian task today is not only to understand the Apocalypse, but to imagine a future that comes after the Apocalypse, to embark onto a relentless fight for the very possibility of a future in the ruins of our present. And this can only start once we understand time as the crucial component of any struggle that wants to be successful in this historic task. While the late global capitalist system is mainly concerned with 'short-termism', what we need is a long-term perspective that will always be governed by the question of what kind of effects our current time – and our own actions – will have not only on the future, but also on the past. Because a future without a witness leaves no one to remember the past.

Unlike the dominant notion of time based on the ideology of 'progress', we need to invent a different temporality – this is the main message of the chapter on the Marshall Islands and the consequences of nuclear testing and nuclear waste – that is able to transmit the 'revelation' into the distant future even if there is no one in the future to receive the warning. The biggest endeavour humanity has ever faced can only be successful if it is grounded in a deep understanding of the eschatological tipping points we are faced with as well as in an unprecedented long-term collective action that is, at the same time, both spatial (local, trans-national, planetary) and temporal (intergenerational solidarity and a commitment to a just and sustainable future that would be evenly distributed across the planet among all species).

Time beyond 'progress' also means the following: on the one hand, we are living on a planet whose history, with the human species as its integral part, goes back 4,567 billion years; on the other hand, it is precisely the human species that can catapult itself – and all other species – into oblivion. When the Doomsday Clock is set only '100 seconds to midnight', it is this time, enormous on the one hand and short on the other, that we need to understand. And instead of being paralyzed by post-apocalyptic melancholy, it is useful to remember Paul Tillich's interpretation of the New Testament's *kairos* as 'the eternal breaking into the temporal'.[26] Instead of believing in the elimination of contingency that is inherent to *chronos* (the invention of the calendar that is measured by 'progress'), we have to rehabilitate the cairologic possibilities. To create a crack in *chronos*-time, through which at least a different end of the world could be imagined and perhaps even constructed, is the main task in the times after the Apocalypse.

Another end of the world is still possible

Thesis 9: Our only choice today is a radical re-invention of the world – or mass extinction.

In the last interview conducted with Günther Anders in 1990 by Konrad Paul Liessmann, thanks to whom we witness a much-needed renewal of interest in his thought, Anders claims that in 1945 only one threat could truly be classified as threatening the end of humanity – namely, nuclear war. 'The fact that today', he says, 'we have many methods with which to commit suicide does not intrinsically alter the fundamental aspects of my analyses of the nuclear situation. But yes, I admit, today we have the choice.'[27]

At the time of this last interview, as worrying as the situation already was, the world hadn't yet reached the eschatological tipping point that we are witnessing today – exactly three decades later. For comparison, while in 2020 the Doomsday Clock was still set to 100 seconds to midnight, in 1990 it was still at 10 minutes to midnight. Even though the collision of the nuclear age and climate crisis had already begun (and continued throughout the intervening decades in the form of ongoing nuclear testings), the 1990s were the years of the 'end of history' – a period that was celebrating the fall of the Iron Curtain and the demise of 'real existing socialism' across the world. Instead of *extinction*, the horizon was still the seemingly never-ending *expansion* of capitalism and 'liberal democracy', representing the final stage of human history. But not even the 'happy' 1990s were evenly distributed; it is sufficient to mention the human victims and massive oils spills created by the war in Kuwait and Iraq, the vast human tragedy in Rwanda or the bloody collapse of Yugoslavia. Then, with the new millennium, came 9/11 – the first big blow to the theory of the 'end of history' – followed by the financial crash of 2007–8, which would lead to a decade of austerity and a decade of protests, including Occupy Wall Street, the so-called 'Arab Spring' and the global climate movement. After a decade of rising inequalities and further expansion of capitalism, already leading to all sorts of morbid symptoms such as authoritarian capitalism and ecofascism, a pandemic hit the globe in 2020, resulting in a radical deepening of our current crisis. During these three decades, from 1990 to 2020, the climate crisis and the nuclear threat didn't disappear; on the contrary, the closer we came to 2020, the more these eschatological threats multiplied and expanded.

As is becoming obvious to millions around the planet,

the current world system, based on endless extraction, exploitation and expansion, is heading towards eschatological tipping points and a situation in which, for instance, nuclear war is even more likely precisely as a result of climate change and the general instability that is reflected not only in the biosphere, but also in the semiosphere, which includes politics and geopolitics as well. And vice versa: the current geopolitical instability and authoritarian- and 'growth'-driven economy are leading to a deepening climate crisis. In other words, the more the current climate crisis worsens, the more critical will be the political and geopolitical tensions that could lead to a much more severe nuclear disaster than Chernobyl, or an even deadlier pandemic, compared to which the current COVID-19 crisis will look just like a footnote to an even bigger tragedy. And the more that politics is still defined in terms of 'there is no alternative' (the notorious politics of TINA), the more our only alternative becomes either a profound social transformation or *extinction*. For what is being 'unveiled' in the years of planetary disaster is the incapability of the current capitalist world system to deal with the multiple and simultaneous eschatological threats that humanity is facing today. In fact, it is precisely this world system that is accelerating and leading towards a nonlinear radical change of the Earth system, which will be irreversible.

Not everything is dark. Even in the midst of our trajectory towards pure nothingness, there is a crack through which light comes in. Even with the post-apocalyptic melancholy spreading faster than a virus, even with the perpetual 'normalization' and introduction of the 'new normal', there is a choice. This is, after all, also the original meaning of the term 'crisis', coming from the Greek word κρίσις ('krisis'). It signifies a turning point provoked by an urgent situation to which we must answer by making a decision or choice.

The year 2020 was such a turning point, catapulting humanity into a future 'after the Apocalypse' in which we were all confronted with a decision: are we going to continue with the so-called 'new normal' of expanding and extractive capitalism that is propelling us towards mass extinction, or are we able and determined enough to reinvent the world in such a way that we can minimize – if not prevent – the eschatological threats (climate crisis, nuclear age, pandemics) that are perhaps still under human control?

As May 2020 was coming to an end, with COVID-19 still on the rampage, the slogan 'ANOTHER END OF THE WORLD IS POSSIBLE' was sprayed in black

Figure 1: Graffiti in Minneapolis, May 2020 (photo by Aren Aizura)

capital letters on a wall in Minneapolis – it appeared after the brutal police murder of George Floyd. It was a version of the future-oriented slogan, 'Another World Is Possible', which became famous during the anti-globalist movement of the 2000s. In only two decades, the *Zeitgeist* has obviously changed: from the hopeful watchword of the World Social Forum, we have finished up with an end-oriented slogan of the last and coming decade. As Pablo Servigne, Raphaël Stevens and Gauthier Chapelle remind us in their recent book, *Another End of the World Is Possible: Living the Collapse (and Not Merely Surviving It)*, a French version of the graffiti had already appeared in 2010 at the University of Nanterre – *Une autre fin du monde est possible*.[28] And regardless of its first origin or location, it is really this slogan that marked the beginning of the decade following the 2007–8 financial crash, a decade full of austerity, rising fascism and global protests, which would bring us to our contemporary moment – the still unfinished year of 2020 in which this message seems to be perfectly capturing our current apocalyptic *Zeitgeist*. The hope (without optimism) that at least a different end might still be possible even in the midst of the COVID-19 pandemic and the virus of structural violence.

The term the French authors propose to deal with the possible global collapse is 'collapsosophy' (from collapse and '-sophy' = wisdom), which departs from the strict domain of science, and comes closer to questions of ethics and emotions, philosophy and metaphysics. Their main project is not only to understand the catastrophes, but to live them, including the sufferings, 'without giving up joy or the possibility of a future'.[29] Unfortunately, it was only as I was finishing this book that I came across Servigne et al.'s work, as well as other recent attempts directed towards not only making sense of the 'Apocalypse', but offering some strategies

in how to deal with it. Besides 'collapsosophy' and
Jean-Pierre Dupuy's 'enlightened doomsaying',[30] one
of the inspiring approaches to the Apocalypse has been
the 'feminist counterapocalypse' as envisaged by Joanna
Zylinska.[31] Even if they don't always build on the work
of Günther Anders, who remains the main influence of
this book, what these projects have in common – and
surely many others I don't mention – is a search for a
new ethics in what Anders called the 'End-Time', or
what I call 'after the Apocalypse'.

The slogan 'Another End of the World is Possible'
that keeps cropping up on walls and streets around the
world perhaps means the following: if the world as we
know it is going to end at some point – be it in 10, 100
or 1,000 years – and it is, in fact, ending every day, it
still doesn't have to end like this. It still doesn't have to
end in suffocation because of a respiratory virus – or by
losing the right to breathe because of the virus of racism
(brutal police murders and structural violence) and
the pandemic of capitalism (air pollution, destruction
of nature, meat consumption, climate crisis). As I will
suggest in the Postscriptum of this book, devoted to the
world after the 'revelation' of COVID-19, the current
pandemic is undoubtedly the most important event of
our times (a truly planetary event that affects everything). But the highest ever recorded temperatures in the
Arctic Circle in late June 2020 or the existing nuclear
threat embodied in the cover of this book (which will
be 'unveiled' in Chapter 3) should cause the same
worldwide attention, determined collective reaction and
unprecedented action as COVID-19 has done. It should
occupy every breath we take, every single thought and
emotion, politics – and ethics. The current pandemic
is not only a consequence of the deteriorating climate
crisis and the destructive relation of humans towards
other species, it is at the same time a 'revelation' about
a much larger catastrophic event that is not only a

much deadlier pandemic yet to come, but the already happening collision of the nuclear age and climate crisis. And this 'revelation', like every revelation, confronts us with a choice. Will we respond to it by further destroying public healthcare systems and sacrificing 'essential workers', by destroying the biosphere and slaughtering animals, by building CyberHouses and CyberTrucks or imagining escapes to Mars and luxury nuclear bunkers in New Zealand, by buying post-apocalyptic products and 'smiling with our eyes' above our fashionable face masks? Or are we going to use our general intellect and imagination, a strong sense of transnational justice and intergenerational solidarity in order to go beyond the Apocalypse, to go beyond the very notion and time of 'progress'?

1

Climate Crisis: Back to the Future Mediterranean

That evening a carpenter knocked on his door and said to him: 'Let me help you build an ark, so that it may become false.' Later a roofer joined them, saying: 'It is raining over the mountains, let me help you, so that it may become false.' Then a helmsman came, wiped the first drop of rain from his hair and said: 'What maps will be of any use tomorrow? I come empty-handed. But let me help you, so that it may become false.

Günther Anders, *Die beweinte Zukunft*, 1961

On the importance of wind

'I never understood wind', said Donald Trump in his winter retreat at Mar-a-Lago in Florida a few days after he became the third president in US history to be impeached, rambling on about wind turbines that he, as if he was a sinister postmodern version of Don Quixote, called 'windmills' that are 'monsters' that 'kill many bald eagles'.[1] He continued: 'You know we have a world, right? So the world is tiny compared to the universe.'[2]

As I was returning back to my seemingly 'tiny' world of my beloved island in the midst of the Adriatic Sea in mid-November 2019, little did I know that Vis[3] would soon be turned into a sort of 'excluded zone', an island separated from the mainland by high waves and wild sea, literally cut off for more than a week because of the one thing Donald Trump obviously doesn't understand – namely, the wind. The coastal city of Split, from where I would take the ferry, packed with tourists during the summer season, felt ghostly and empty. But luckily, it was just the usual Mediterranean autumn *spleen*. Split wasn't flooded yet. It wasn't radioactive. Coronavirus hadn't yet arrived.

In fact, *jugo* (literally meaning 'southern'), which is as different from a refreshing wind as it can get, never felt so good – like a breeze of relief on the deck of the ferry *Petar Hektorović*,[4] which was just departing from Split to the island of Vis during that windy warm autumn evening. But as everyone from the Mediterranean knows, wind can often trick you. As the lights from the coast were disappearing in the night, a full moon emerged above the horizon and the waves were already playing with the ferry, always getting stronger as we approach the open sea.

During summer, this characteristic south and southeast Mediterranean wind usually lasts for several days, but during its peak in November it doesn't stop for more than ten continuous days. If you happen to experience *jugo* for the very first time, you might even come to think it is a pleasant wind. During summer it creates unusually high waves (sometimes turning into a wind locally known as *garbin*), while the air remains hot as if there was no wind at all. But if you ever experienced *jugo* for a longer period, especially during late autumn, when the relentless howling causes a peculiar state of mind, then it can become quite an unpleasant experience. Originating in the Sahara Desert, during winter it brings more rainfall and higher waves, usually speeding up to 100 kilometres per hour, and continuing for days with the same strength, sometimes even reaching hurricane speeds in North Africa and Southern Europe. It doesn't come suddenly; it blows continuously, getting stronger day by day, accompanied by low dark-grey clouds and sometimes thunder, turning into a storm after the third day.

Due to the humidity, low barometric pressure, grey skies and storms, *jugo* became so notorious that during the time of the Republic of Dubrovnik (originally named the Republic of Ragusa, which existed from 1358 until 1808), a special law was introduced stating that no Council sessions, decisions or laws were allowed to take place during the *južina*. The south wind brought politics to a standstill for as long as it continued to blow. Even crimes that were committed during heavy southerly winds were treated with more leniency.

From today's perspective, this might sound as if Dubrovnik was really a city from *The Game of Thrones* (as most of the contemporary tourists perceive it and travel there precisely in order to see this fictional location), but the original history of the Republic of Ragusa was way more interesting than any Hollywood fantasy. For centuries and even millennia, there was a rich vernacular culture and knowledge in the Mediterranean – overwritten, in the meantime, by the history of nation-states, global tourism or the film industry – that was very well aware that wind can not only determine whether rain will fall, but it can also affect people's mood or health and, as the Republic of Ragusa and other cities on both sides of the Adriatic Sea, including Venice or Naples, knew very well, it is a wind that might even lead you to commit a crime – or suicide.

Probably one of the best descriptions of *sirocco* comes from a Scottish traveller who visited Italy in the eighteenth century and published a book called *A Tour through Sicily and Malta, in a Series of Letters to William Beckford, Esq., of Semrly in Suffolk* (1773). When he was in the Province of Naples, the wind had already been blowing for six days without intermission and 'has indeed blown away all our gaiety and spirits; and if it continues much longer', he added, 'I do not know what may be the consequence'.[5] Then he mentions a story about a Parisian marquis who had been there ten days earlier and was so full of 'animal spirits' that the people thought he was mad:

> He never remained a moment in the same place; but, at their grave conversations, used to skip from room to room with such amazing elasticity, that the Italians swore he had got springs in his shoes. I met him this morning, walking with the step of a philosopher; a smelling bottle in his hands, and all his vivacity extinguished. I asked him what was the matter? 'Ah, *mon ami*,' said he, 'I am near to death. I, who never knew the meaning of the word *ennui. Mais cet execrable vent*, if it lasts even two days more, I will hang myself.'[6]

Perhaps this is the best description of *sirocco*. In short, if you don't kill someone, you might end up killing yourself. And there might even be a pharmacological explanation to it. When in the mid-1970s an Israeli pharmacologist named Felix Sulman began testing the urine of people who were particularly bothered by the blowing of the *sharav*, the Israeli version of *sirocco*, he found out that those people who suffered from nausea, migraines, irritability and insomnia just before and after the *sharav* exhibited a tenfold increase in their serotonin levels. The hot dry wind (*sharav*) led to increased degrees of ionization in the atmosphere, which, as a result, induced a higher serotonin release.[7] While serotonin is usually associated with inducing a sense of happiness, too much serotonin obviously creates the opposite effect – melancholy, and even *ennui* – as the Parisian in Naples knew very well. But it's not just a crazy marquis; obviously, we are all 'weather-sensitive' individuals.

For centuries and even thousands of years, people had a shared knowledge about the climate and weather patterns in the Mediterranean, understanding it as something that has not just psychical effects but also deep psychological consequences. Wind was – and still is, whatever Donald Trump thinks about it – much more than just wind. The settlements of ancient cities across the Mediterranean, from Egypt to the Adriatic islands, were positioned and built not only with the wind itself in mind, but with how wind and climate affects agriculture, where exactly to cultivate olive trees or wine, how to navigate the seas. It was a sort of 'place-making' that was taking into account climate disruptions, from floods to drought.

Our ancestors didn't only know that, without the wind – this extraordinary circulatory system of our planet connecting climate and cultures, languages and emotions – the Earth would be uninhabitable. They were also aware that the wind – just like the sea, or the atmosphere, the stars and planets – was something more than just moving air. Maybe they still didn't know how to explain the ionization of the atmosphere and the role of serotonin, but they knew very well that *sirocco*, or any other wind, certainly has effects on the population, agriculture, economy, society, psychology – and on the future itself.

If there was a wind in November coming from the south, besides implementing special 'wind laws', the place-makers of ancient coastal cities knew that huge waves, rainfalls and high tides were coming too. In other words, 'place-making' didn't only depend on merely predicting the weather, but on knowing and understanding the climate, this ultimate system of complexities. Today, this knowledge, at least when it comes to most of the world's governments and populist leaders, seems to be forgotten – or they simply care more about extraction and expansion of capital than about the future of the planet, global warming and rising sea levels.

When we read Donald Trump's ramblings about the wind ('I never understood wind'), it seems we are once again back with that unfortunate Libyan tribe that literally declared war on the wind, as described in the famous passage from Herodotus' *Histories* (written some two and a half thousand years ago) and retold by Ralph Fiennes in the romantic war drama film *The English Patient* (1996):

> On the borders of the Nasamones is the country of the Psylli, who perished in this wise: the force of the south wind dried up their water-tanks, and all their country, lying within the region of the Syrtis, was waterless. Taking counsel together they marched southwards (I tell the story as it is told by the Libyans), and when they came into the sandy desert a strong south wind buried them. So they perished utterly, and the Nasamones have their country.[8]

If we don't want to end up like this Libyan tribe that marched against the *ghibli* (the Libyan word for the southern wind), we have to understand the importance of the wind. The very fact that the word for *sirocco* still exists in so many languages across the Mediterranean, *jugo* in Croatian, *levante* in Spain, *leveche* in Morocco, *chergui* in Algeria, *chili* in Tunisia, *ghibli* in Libya, *khamsin* in Egypt, *sharav* in Israel, *sharkiye* in Jordan, and *shamal* in Iraq, shows the importance of this knowledge-system that is today turned into a sort of vernacular. It shows the importance of knowing something such as – the wind. When Donald Trump, as a sort of cynical version of Don Quixote, attacked 'windmills' in order to defend the perverted ideal of 'bald eagles' as the symbol of the (fossil fuel-driven) United States, he was marching his armies not only against nature itself, but also against this knowledge that was constructed through millennia in order to avert the fate of the Libyan tribe that utterly perished. Only this time, if we don't take climate crisis seriously, there will be no Nasamonians coming after.

Solastalgia for the Mediterranean

As *jugo* was blowing from the south across the Adriatic Sea above the island of Vis, I was probably – in a quite naive and romantic way – still thinking that there is no better place to write about the 'End-Time' than on a remote island during winter. Sometimes it feels as if you are, indeed, in a place at the end of times. And it is not so much the place that is affected; it is time that transforms itself. It becomes 'slower' (in Vis it is the philosophy of *pomalo*); or, rather, the clock-time universe becomes less important than in the prevailing speed of the *chronos*-time world, which follows the 24/7 rhythm of capitalism connected to work, schedules and timetables.

Summer, at least in the so-called Northern hemisphere, since the creation of modern mass tourism in the nineteenth century, was the 'place' (or rather the time) where people – usually the privileged – would live in the 'here and now', not thinking about yesterday or tomorrow. All that matters is being able to take your time and break free, as much as you can, from your daily duties and worries, away from the overwhelming capitalist 24/7 temporality connected to schedules, never-ending online meetings, daily work, commuting,

Figure 2: Italy in 2100. Jay Simons, 2012

flights, paying bills, social networks, stress, anxiety, traffic, noise, news, wars, elections, violence, insecurity, virus – and last, but not least, fears about the end of the world.

But what if, suddenly, during that moment of tranquillity and summer peace, something unexpected happens, something that ruins the carefree 'here and now' like a flashback coming not from the past, but from the future? What if a certain nostalgia for that precious present moment is being born – not simply nostalgia for the past, but an unusual sort of sentiment towards the present that is unfolding relentlessly and becoming the past – or rather a memory in the future.

Like that moment with my friends at our favourite ŽŽ *konoba* in Komiža singing out loud some old music hits, in a tiny room that could just as well have been a whole universe, dancing and celebrating as if there were no yesterday and no tomorrow. The night just started and it might, perhaps, never ever end. It might, as well, be a party at the end of the world. And it wouldn't matter. But at a certain point, in a moment of utter *jouissance* (because it's joyful and painful at the same time, too much to endure ...), I start longing for this present before it's gone. The present is already a memory, even if I am still here in the 'present', I am already transposed into the future from where I look upon the unfolding present as something that is already past.

Or like a moment from last summer, when my mother, watching the shining full moon quickly emerging above Mount Hum, tells her young grandchild: 'This is us, and that is the moon, see how quickly we move,' – and I, as his uncle and her child, even more quickly transform into the curious grandchild myself, seeing the moon for the first time, not just as the moon, but seeing ourselves in the reflection of the Moon: three generations watching the 4.53 billion-year-old moon, how it rises above the hill above the island above us. And I become fully aware of this moment, of this present that is vanishing as quickly as the moon is moving.

And what about the vanishing coastal towns and cities themselves, their languages and cultures, their places and histories? What if 'the Mediterranean as it used to be' (incidentally, one of the slogans of Croatia's tourist office a few years ago) is already unrecognizable in the coming decades, by which time the sea will have submerged most of the places? What about the lemons and figs, the olives and donkeys, rosemary and oregano, the wines and the songs that have for millennia inhabited the Mediterranean region, that was so alluringly described by the great scholars Fernand Braudel and Predrag Matvejević?[9] And what about the sea itself, its flora and fauna, its rhythm and memories?

I think about that often as I swim in the Adriatic Sea around the islands of Vis and Biševo, whose form today is itself the result of a gigantic catastrophe that happened some 220 million years ago when the dinosaurs still ruled the Earth.[10] During that time, deep beneath the place where tourists swim today, there was an active volcano and, if you know how to look – or someone from the locals points you in the right direction – you can still see petrified lava, volcanic bombs, ash, salt and sedimentary rocks around the beaches of Komiža. Millions of years are unveiling (Apocalypse in the sense of 'revelation' visible in geology) themselves here in this little paradise in the midst of the Adriatic Sea, including the extinction of dinosaurs, the evolution of first primates and first flowering plants, leading to the diversification of mammals and, finally, to the evolution of humans who are now swimming peacefully as if 'paradise' wasn't a result of a previous enormous catastrophe. Or as if another catastrophe wasn't unfolding at this very moment.

While most of the tourists who jump into the sea from sailing boats and yachts see the beauty of what they perceive as 'paradise' without really knowing that they are just lucky enough to be experiencing the results of a previous major catastrophe, scientists see microplastics that are polluting our seas. Where the carefree visitor sees crystal clear water and picturesque vineyards, the local population sees a diminishing stock of fish and the fruits of their hard work possibly ruined because, once again, there had been no rain for months on the islands, or there was just another sudden fierce storm. Even before the first ancient Greek colonies on *Issa* (today, Vis) and *Pharos* (today, Hvar), for more than two millennia, the populations of these islands successfully withstood wars of colonization – and the weather as well. However, what is happening today is not yet another disaster or slow degradation of the environment; it is a profound change that might mean the end of the Mediterranean as it has existed so far, a change that is visible also on the island of Vis.

Unlike many other places in the world, the islands of the Adriatic Sea are still not threatened by rapid sea-level rises or devastating storms, but the point is the following: the record-breaking summer temperatures, stronger winds and extreme weather in the Mediterranean in recent years could be understood as a 'revelation' of things to come. All these changes leave a visible mark not only on the surface of the island or in the sea; they also affect human subjectivity and lead to nostalgia for something that is disappearing – not for the past itself, but for the present that will no longer exist in the future.

In order to describe this unique feeling of longing for the present, this sort of 'anticipatory nostalgia', the Australian environmental philosopher Glenn Albrecht, after studying the effects of long-term drought and large-scale mining activity on communities in New South Wales, coined the term 'solastalgia'.[11] It comes from the Latin word *sōlācium* (comfort) and the Greek root -*algia* (pain), describing a new sort of 'homesickness' that is focused not so much just on the place as it has been (the return to 'home'), but on the place at its moment of disappearance. Solastalgia, according to Albrecht, describes the sense of pain that is experienced by 'people who strongly empathize with the idea that the earth is their home'[12] and who find witnessing the destruction of the earth distressing. 'There is an increase in ecosystem distress syndromes', warns Albrecht, 'matched by a corresponding increase in human distress syndromes.'[13]

Unlike the original meaning of nostalgia, coming from the Greek *nóstos* (Homeric word meaning 'home coming') and *álgos* (meaning 'pain'), this distinctive form of contemporary 'homesickness' is not merely nostalgia towards a place called 'home', as a fixed point in the past. It is a longing for the place that is changing in 'real time', a longing that is connected to some sort of nostalgia, but, unlike traditional nostalgia, it is fundamentally future-oriented. There is no 'return' (as in nostalgia) to the place in the future, because the future itself is in question. The human reaction to this irreversibility is what we could call solastalgia.

And, indeed, all across the planet, not only in communities that have already been hit by major climate disruptions, but also in the seemingly protected castles of the privileged West, solastalgia is becoming a new predominant feeling. Those at the climate 'frontline', like indigenous communities or those whose lives were already devastated by wild storms or rising sea levels, were the first to experience this sort of emotional trauma and very often, faced with the struggle for mere survival, they didn't have the luxury to even contemplate any sort of *-algia*. Then came the scientists, the 'frontline' workers who were researching the areas and were continuously warning of already existing disastrous consequences of climate crisis. In October 2019, in the same month that Extinction Rebellion activists staged a funeral for the planet in central London and talked about 'connecting with our grief', leading researchers of climate change published a letter in the journal *Science* titled 'Grieving environmental scientists need support'.

In the letter, they warned that many scientists experience 'strong grief responses' that can no longer be ignored.[14] The problem is what they call the 'pervasive illusion' that scientists must be 'dispassionate observers'.[15] In opposition to that, what we need today is acknowledgement of the fact that very often it is precisely climate scientists who are some sort of 'frontline workers' (a term that became famous with the coronavirus pandemic, but should also be applied to all who are working on the frontlines of climate crisis) whose very object of research can be defined by loss. As the lead author of the letter and marine biologist Tim Gordon says:

> We're documenting the destruction of the world's most beautiful and valuable ecosystems, and it's impossible to remain emotionally detached. When you spend your life studying places like the Great Barrier Reef or the Arctic ice caps, and then watch them bleach into rubble fields or melt into the sea, it hits you hard.[16]

He added that if we are 'serious about finding any sort of future for our natural ecosystems', what is necessary is to 'avoid getting trapped in cycles of grief. We need to allow ourselves to cry – and then see beyond our tears'.[17]

The general conclusion of the environmental scientists' warning is that, instead of ignoring or suppressing grief, they should be acknowledging, accepting and working through it. In other words, it is not just OK to cry, it is necessary. But what if, instead of grief and mourning, what is being born at the 'frontlines' of climate crisis – among indigenous communities and 'frontline' workers, among people losing their homes, their loved ones, their habitat and future – is rather a sort of 'post-apocalyptic melancholy'? If mourning usually means being able to transcend loss through an adaptive strategy enabling a 'return to normal', for 'post-apocalyptic melancholy' it is precisely the 'normal' that is part of the pathology. And it is in this sense that this sort of melancholy – the inability and often even unwillingness to go beyond the loss and 'return to normal' – can have another function. It is not just grief over the lost past but a sort of 'anticipatory grief' that could help us navigate through the present and perhaps prevent the loss that will have happened if we stay trapped in cycles of grieving the loss that in fact can never be overcome.

What if, today, instead of being nostalgic towards the present that is already gone (solastalgia) and treating mourning as the 'normal' response to loss, we embrace the melancholy that is usually portrayed as 'pathological'? What if 'post-apocalyptic melancholy' can serve as a sort of strategy that would insist precisely on not coming to terms with the loss and would thus, instead of mourning the past, actually mourn the future itself in order to prevent it from becoming true? The first dictum of this strategy is – there is no 'return to normality'. There is no 'returning home' (*nóstos*), and the only nostalgia that perhaps still carries a subversive potential is a nostalgia for the future, a sort of anticipatory strategy that would treat the loss as something that will have happened – if we don't already mourn it today. And here melancholy comes back into play, because we must know that even if we mourn the future today, it might not avert the loss.

This strategy comes closest to a moving story about Noah written by Günther Anders in 1961 under the title *Die beweinte Zukunft* ('The Cried-For Future', or rather 'Mourned Future') that was recently rediscovered by the French philosopher Jean-Pierre Dupuy in his project of construction of a philosophy of 'enlightened doomsaying'.[18] It is a version of the famous biblical flood story, but what makes it relevant for our contemporary time, which seems to be stuck in cycles of grief, is the future perfect, or *futur antérieur*, that Noah used in order to describe a future that will have happened – namely, the flood. Of course, no one believed the prophet of doom and his warnings, people turned a blind eye and everyone was tired of Noah and 'his' flood. Yet, Noah insisted that the coming flood was 'their' (flood) as well. What drove him mad was the inevitable future, so in order to warn those who didn't

believe him, he invented a strategy to turn the catastrophe into something that had already happened.
Although only a man mourning the death of a beloved
person was allowed to do this, Noah clothed himself in
sackcloth and covered his head with ashes. 'Clothed in
the garb of truth', as a 'bearer of sorrow', he returned to
the city where soon a crowd of curious people gathered
around him. They wondered whether someone had
died and who the dead person was. He told them that
many had died and that they themselves were dead as
well. The people didn't believe him. But he certainly got
their attention. When they asked him when this catastrophe had taken place, he replied: 'Tomorrow.' As the
gathering crowd became even more confused, Noah
said these words:

> The day after tomorrow, the flood will be something
> that will have been. And when the flood will have been,
> everything that is will never have existed. When the
> flood will have carried off everything that is, everything
> that will have been, it will be too late to remember, for
> there will no longer be anyone alive. And so there will
> no longer be any difference between the dead and those
> who mourn them. If I have come before you, it is in
> order to reverse time, to mourn tomorrow's dead today.
> The day after tomorrow it will be too late.[19]

I recently discovered a video from 1987 showing
Günther Anders reading *Die beweinte Zukunft* in his
Vienna apartment, where he would die only a few
years later. Originally, it was a story written in 1961,
three years after his visit to Hiroshima and one year
after the publication of his correspondence with the
so-called 'Hiroshima-pilot' Claude Eatherly. In the
video recording, Anders reveals that his Noah's ark
story wouldn't have been written if he hadn't received
a letter from an unknown young woman who wrote to

him after reading his books. This woman was Gudrun Ensslin, later famous as a member of the Rote Armee Fraktion, whom he never met. Listening to Anders reading the story about Noah one year after Chernobyl, a decade after the so-called 'German Autumn' and after the time when the antiwar movement was turning (among other directions) towards terrorism, we find ourselves immersed in a world that was already quite apocalyptic and heading towards our current historic moment. If we take Anders's philosophy of catastrophe seriously, what is unfolding in Noah's story is nothing but a mourning for our own future. Not for the flood to come, but for the flood that will have been.

'Normalization' of the Apocalypse

To reverse time in the sense of mourning tomorrow's dead seems even more difficult today than in the late twentieth century of Günther Anders. It is so because the very object of mourning, namely the unprecedented loss, is so big that its scale is becoming impossible to grasp ('supraliminal'). In the early twenty-first century, climate crisis is accelerating so rapidly that even the most pessimistic global scenarios – for instance, the calculation by the United Nations' Inter-governmental Panel on Climate Change that, by the year 2100, waters of the Mediterranean will rise by more than a metre – now seem quite optimistic. And as soon as you start to get used to the 'new normal', there is already a further study that corrects what was essentially a data error in previous calculations and that basically makes mourning itself impossible because the very object of loss is constantly changing and rising.

That is exactly what happened in late October 2019 when such a paper was published in *Nature Communications* showing that there was in fact a miscalculation in the previous reports, and that roughly three times as many people are at risk by 2050 because of rising sea levels – which would mean quite literally the erasure of the world's great coastal cities, including most of the cities on the coasts of the Mediterranean.[20] According to this new study, around 150 million people are currently living on land that will find itself below the high-tide line in just 30 years. And that's the hopeful scenario, where warming remains no higher than 2°C and the ice sheets don't collapse. In a more pessimistic scenario, there might be as many as 300 million people who will have to flee their flooded lands by 2050.[21] According to another recent study, up to 630 million people – most of them in Asia – will be threatened by flooding from sea-level rises by the end of the century.[22]

Then, as if this terrible news wasn't enough, another study was published in November 2019 by an Oxford physical climate scientist that painted another rather bleak future for the Mediterranean. This time, it is because the rapidly melting Arctic ice, seemingly far away, is disturbing the jet stream that, combined with climate change, can cause truly extreme weather events. Many of the most recent computer models predict that the jet will shift a little towards the pole, which would result in a greater influence of the tropics. What would that actually mean for the region still known as the Mediterranean? The study describes how

> we should expect to see the warm, dry regions at the edge of the tropics extend a little further out from the equator. The strongest impacts of this would likely be felt in regions such as the Mediterranean, which are already highly sensitive to fluctuations in rainfall. A northward jet shift would act to steer much needed rainstorms towards central Europe instead, leaving the Mediterranean at greater risk of drought.[23]

The present-day Mediterranean, which geologically dates back to the earliest days of the evolution of our planet, is obviously undergoing such a profound – even geological – change that it doesn't represent just an environmental problem, but also a humanitarian problem of unprecedented proportions, which will require a complete transformation of the way we manage societies, including urban planning and place making, the economy and the very understanding of 'progress' and 'growth'. It literally means that major coastal cities across the world, from Mumbai to Shanghai, from Bangkok to Alexandria, will soon be under water. Climate crisis is also threatening some of the Mediterranean's most historical sites, from Dubrovnik and Venice to the ancient Basilica in the Italian city of Aquileia and the ancient Phoenician metropolis of Tyre. According to a recent study published in *Nature Communications*, more than 90 per cent of the region's World Heritage sites – some of the oldest remaining signs of the history of human civilization – are at risk from sea-level rise and coastal erosion.[24]

Then there is another piece of recent research that might be described as a truly dystopian 'new normal'. It suggests that the scale of plastic pollution in our oceans could be a million times worse than previously recorded. What really surprised the biological oceanographer Jennifer Brandon, who led this research, published in the science journal *Limnology and Oceanography Letters*, was that 'every salp, regardless of year collected, species, life stage, or part of the ocean collected, had plastics in its stomach'.[25] The problem with that is not just that fish are already full of plastics, but that microplastics are subsequently entering the food chain, which means that, in the end, humans themselves are eating it. Where does it come from? More than one-third of the microplastics in the oceans come from the textile industry, from synthetic fabrics such as polyester or

nylon. Car tyres are the second-highest source, releasing
plastic particles as they erode.[26] According to a recent
study about human consumption of microplastics,
published in 2019 in the journal *Environmental Science
and Technology*, the average person today eats at least
50,000 particles of microplastic a year and breathes in
a similar quantity.[27] This is what a perfect suicidal circle
of capitalist expansion looks like.

Having these dark future scenarios as our only
horizon, as a future that will have been, solastalgia
doesn't appear just as an individual sentiment anymore;
it is not just a personal emotional response to the
uncertainty over the future that was repressed for so
long. What we have at play here is, rather, a return
of the repressed that is provoking a sort of planetary
'post-apocalyptic melancholy'. It is 'post-apocalyptic'
not only because the Apocalypse as 'revelation' already
happened, it is 'post-apocalyptic' also because the loss
is so big that it is becoming impossible to cope with it.
And the scale of this loss is constantly growing. Namely,
the impacts of global warming and other eschatological
'tipping points' (which will be explored in the following
chapters of this book) will not only undermine basic
rights to life, water, food and housing for billions of
people, but also democracy itself – those with power
and money will segregate whole populations, as in the
times of racial and colonial apartheid. In fact, in June
2019 the UN Special Rapporteur on extreme poverty
and human rights, Philip Alston, warned that the world
is increasingly at risk of 'climate apartheid'. According
to the report, even in the best-case scenario of a 1.5°C
temperature increase by 2100, extreme temperatures in
many regions will have disastrous consequences on food
security and 'it could push more than 120 million more
people into poverty by 2030'.[28] In such a situation, many
will have to choose between starvation and migration,
which would lead to a 'climate apartheid' scenario

'where the wealthy pay to escape overheating, hunger and conflict while the rest of the world is left to suffer'.[29]

The island of Vis is luckily not yet affected by such disastrous changes or catastrophic events that have already devastated many other places across the world, mainly in Africa and Asia, but this is where solastalgia comes into play: we do not need to imagine how the Mediterranean will look in the future, it is sufficient to look into the present to find the future already here. The seas are already getting warmer, and even if the fish are not yet extinct, they are already full of microplastics. Sometimes disaster comes rapidly and leaves a horrific mark, as in the case of the deadly tsunami that hit Sri Lanka in December 2004, or the Australian bushfires of 2019/2020; sometimes it develops like a 'slow motion' movie and gradually transforms what we understand as 'normality'. In the Mediterranean in November 2019, disaster came in the form of a sudden flood that rose several times then disappeared, a quick but calamitous 'revelation' about the coming future.

The flood, another recent warning of the ultimate flood Anders was writing about in his 'Mourned Future', hit the Mediterranean as if someone had suddenly pushed a 'fast forward' button not so much into a distant future but into a dystopian present. And as the *jugo* was relentlessly blowing over the island of Vis, the signal on my mobile phone was suddenly lost. Instead of the future Mediterranean predicted by the climate scientists or the flood that Noah was warning us about, I was suddenly back to this reality: the flood of November 2019. The Internet was, luckily, still working, and I soon realized that the ferry, the same good old *Petar Hektorović* that brought me to the island and always brings me here, was stranded ashore due to the gust of the mighty wind. Then it became quite obvious even to me, still writing in the safety of a tiny home, that the sea was too wild and that the island had, in the meantime, become a sort of

Figure 3: #NoEsFuegoEsCapitalismo, by Elijo Dignidad (www.elijodignidad.org)

'excluded zone' without any ferry or boat connections to the mainland. I found myself in the midst of a storm in the midst of the Adriatic Sea.

During one week, all boat connections to the islands were shut down, the waves were abnormally high and the wind recorded at Mount Hum on Vis, which I could see from my writing desk, was as strong as 152 km/h. It was the strongest *jugo* ever recorded in Croatia, with the highest ever wave hitting the coast of the Adriatic Sea recorded in the waters of Dubrovnik (10.87 metres high),[30] and the highest tide recorded in Split (91.1 centimetres), which flooded the historic cellars of Diocletian's Palace, the ancient substructures listed by UNESCO as a World Heritage Site. In the times of the emperor Diocletian, the sea level was nearly 2 metres lower than it is today, so with a high tide of 91.1 centimetres, it makes it almost 3 metres higher compared to the times when the place was originally built in the fourth century.

However, even in times of exceptionally high tides, the ancient place-makers would still be able to protect the coastal cities or find mechanisms, like Venice did for centuries, to reduce the intensity of the high tide or construct substructures and superstructures that would be able to withhold even the highest tide. The Venetians, as part of the Mediterranean culture that for millennia cherished and circulated knowledge about the sea and the wind, knew that *sirocco* combined with a rising tide can cause the *acqua alta* ('high water') in the Venetian Lagoon.

But then came November 2019. As the thunderous wind was blowing over Vis, I was reading the first warnings that Venice could be hit by an exceptional high tide. The wind that was blowing over islands was heading towards the so-called 'pearl of the Adriatic'. And then, finally, the exceptionally intense *acqua alta* peaked at 1.87 metres on 12 November 2019, and left post-apocalyptic images of Venice even before the next two high tides would hit again. With three tides above 140 centimetres in just one week, 2019 became the worst year for high tides in Venice since 1872, when official tide statistics were first produced.[31] A fatal combination of factors produced the flooding disaster in Venice: in addition to *sirocco* and huge waves, coastal flooding was exacerbated by abnormally high tides caused by a full moon and elevated sea levels from low atmospheric pressure. But it would be a mistake to call it just a 'natural' catastrophe.

In a quite dark ironic twist, which would in religious times probably be interpreted as a 'sign from the heavens', as the politicians of the Italian regional council located on Venice's Grand Canal were debating the 2020 budget and deciding to reject measures on climate change, the water had already started to penetrate the council chamber in Ferro Fini Palace, once one of the most elegant hotels in Venice, built in the seventeenth century. Very soon, the building was flooded for the very first time in its history. A few moments later, Andrea Zanoni, deputy chairman of the environment committee, wrote in a Facebook post, which was accompanied by photographs of that same room under water: 'Ironically, the chamber was flooded two minutes after the majority League, Brothers of Italy, and Forza Italia parties rejected our amendments to tackle climate change.'[32]

The disastrous *acqua alta* that hit Venice in November 2019 – not just once, but three times – was obviously not only a product of climate change and a fatal combination of different factors that reinforce each other, but also a result of human mismanagement, or, more precisely, corruption. The multibillion-euro project to protect Venice from flooding under the acronym MOSE (quite ironically, alluding to the biblical character Moses), has been under construction since 2003 and has been delayed a number of times. And even if it is constructed, it will be insufficient, given that it was planned on a scenario of sea levels in the northern Adriatic rising only 22 centimetres by 2100, which, according to all current calculations, remains quite an optimistic assumption.[33] It is no wonder that Reuters featured an article with the headline: 'Venice still waiting for Moses to hold back the seas.'[34] In other words, the giant engineering project once intended to save Venice was planned for a world that no longer exists.

Today, when new catastrophes and disasters are occupying our most recent memory, the floods of November 2019 perhaps still serve as a sort of Noah's warning for the local communities that are becoming aware that they will have to become accustomed to floods as a 'normal' part of life in the Mediterranean. This capacity to endure in spite of difficulties is usually called 'resilience', but it would be better to call it the 'normalization' of the Apocalypse, to understand it as a process through which something that is not 'normal' becomes 'normal' or even 'natural'.

An illustration of this 'normalization' came on the same day that Venice suffered its worst flooding for 50 years. Even though the city still hadn't recovered from the first record-breaking *acqua alta* and was still facing two more high tides, the machine of 'global tourism' had to continue operating. Usually, the ideology that supports and produces 'normalization' can easily be discerned in the mainstream media aimed at the broadest audience of possible consumers. For instance, the very same day of the floods, the British *Telegraph* published an article in its 'Travel / Destinations' section with the following headline: 'Can I still visit Venice after the worst floods in 50 years?'[35] The answer is, of course, 'yes': 'In fact, some tourists deliberately travel to Venice during this time of the year to witness the annual high tides, or the *acqua alta*.'[36]

In another illustration of mainstream 'normalization', the UK tabloid newspaper *The Sun* published travel advice with the following headline: 'Is Venice safe? What to do if you've booked a holiday to the flooded city as state of emergency is declared.' But why am I quoting such a newspaper as *The Sun*? Precisely because, through the mass market circulation of (precisely tabloid) ideas, we can detect the prevailing ideology or market interests. The article first describes the 'terrifying images' of 'tourists walking the deep water as many of the popular attractions in the Italian city are at risk of facing irreversible damage', and holidaymakers who 'have been wading through thigh-high water to snap selfies of themselves in front of flooded buildings and deserted squares'.[37] But then it quickly states that Venice is also very used to dealing with flooding and that, even while many of the tourist attractions, cafes and restaurants are closed, some have remained open, including the Ducal Palace. At the end of the 'travel advice', there is total relief: 'Flights are still operational between the UK and Venice.'[38]

As frescoes dating back to the Renaissance were endangered by the salty sea water, specialized art magazines were reporting that 'despite catastrophic flooding, much of Venice's Art appears safe for the moment', with relief evident in the subtitle: 'Major institutions, as well as the Venice Biennale, are reporting some welcome good news.'[39] The article noted that the Venice Biennale, in particular, fared remarkably well. Despite forecasts predicting continued flooding until 16 November, the Arsenale and Giardini reopened to the public two days earlier, clocking up an impressive 2,582 visitors by closing time.

In short, the world's leading newspapers, the tourist industry and the arts industry were doing what they always did and what they would be doing again very soon during the COVID-19 pandemic – just take the case of Austria's 'Ibiza of the Alps' ski resort covering up an initial case of COVID-19 that would spread throughout Europe.[40] However, this process of covering up the disaster in order to 'save the economy' wasn't particularly new. Thomas Mann had already described it in *Death in Venice*, published just before the outbreak of the First World War, where the authorities are covering up a cholera outbreak so that the tourist machine could continue operating:

> In early June the quarantine barracks of the hospital had been filling silently, in the two orphanages there was no longer enough room, and a horrific traffic developed between the city and San Michele. But the fear of general damage, regard for the recently opened exhibition of paintings in the municipal gardens, for the enormous financial losses that threatened the tourist industry in case of a panic, had more impact in the city than love of truth and observation of international agreements.[41]

However, there is an important difference between Thomas Mann's dystopian Venice and our current post-apocalyptic reality. What the floods in Venice 2019, and only a couple of months later the coronavirus pandemic, unveiled is not only how fear of 'general damage', all those opened exhibitions and financial losses for the tourist industry, once again become more important than the well-being of people or places itself. These eschatological threats (both the floods and the virus) also showed how quickly things return to 'normal' or, more precisely, how a 'new normal' is always being constructed in the ruins of the old order, how the disorder very often ends up being turned into 'things as usual' (as long as the flights are not interrupted and art museums can be visited, everything must still be OK).

The flooding of Venice in November 2019, only a few months before the whole city would be in quarantine due to the coronavirus pandemic, showed a clear paradigm shift in our understanding of the catastrophe itself: what if, instead of fearing the disaster, we have become – or rather have been forced to become – accustomed to the disaster? What if the crowd described in Anders's story about Noah is becoming even more blind – *Apokalypseblindheit* is a term Anders would use to describe this – than ever before? And what if it was exactly the floods in Venice that revealed that most contemporary disasters are anything but 'natural' catastrophes? In order to reverse time in the sense of mourning tomorrow's dead today (including the death of Venice), what is required, besides a mental jump into the *futur antérieur* where the flood 'will have been', is a deeper understanding of our contemporary moment as a highly political one in which the Apocalypse is already provoking a struggle for meaning that very often ends up in the 'normalization' of the catastrophe. 'Normalization' is not merely the process of humans adopting to a situation after the disaster; it is much more an ideological process through which the very abnormality of a given situation is being transformed into something that is now described as the 'new normal'.

Death of Venice

Even though numerous towns and cities across the Mediterranean coast witnessed heavy flooding during that November 2019, how come it was precisely the post-apocalyptic images of Venice that captured popular imagination? Where does this centuries-old fascination with the so called 'Queen of the Adriatic' come from? Is it a fascination just with any sinking city, or is it a fascination with cities, like Venice, with so many layers of history, historic architecture and precious art treasures? Or is it, if you think about the numerous Asian and African cities that are continuously faced with much more devastating floods, simply eurocentrism?

What we obviously have unfolding here is a struggle for meaning. Disaster always generates meaning. As a rule, this meaning is a reflection of the state of society in which disaster occurs, and very often this meaning is highly ideological. For instance, when Venice was submerged in water, the *Washington Post* published an article under the title 'Venice floods threaten priceless artwork and history – and a unique way of life'.[42] At first glance, nothing seems wrong with this title. As we know, Venice, named a UNESCO World Heritage Site back in 1987, is home not only to historic basilicas and architecture, but also to priceless works of art by such Renaissance masters as Titian, Tintoretto and Giorgione. But doesn't this sort of reaction to flooded Venice contain an underlying eurocentric construction of Venice as a place with 'priceless artwork and history' and 'a unique way of life', in contrast to places without 'priceless artwork and history' and 'a unique way of life' – which nevertheless, even if Titian is not in their museums, should be saved as well? Obviously, even in times of a planetary crisis, what persists is a certain eurocentric blindness towards the history, culture and arts of other endangered places that don't belong to the Western popular imagination or set of values. Even if 25–30 million people in Bangladesh are forced to relocate because of climate change over the next 50 years (which is probably already an outdated estimation),[43] why was it just Venice that occupied the headlines as a place threatened by the flood? When climate crisis – including much more devastating floods than the one that hit the Mediterranean in November 2019 – affects Africa and Asia the most, how come it is still Europe's disasters that seem to be attracting more attention?

A similar misplacement of empathy happened during another event, in April 2019, when the famous Notre-Dame de Paris caught fire. The *New York Times* immediately published a headline saying: 'Fire at

Notre-Dame Cathedral leads to expressions of heart-break across the world.'[44] The article observed that the fire that tore through Notre-Dame 'generated an outpouring of grief in France and around the world as the symbol of French culture and history burned'.[45] It's not necessary to be versed in the critique of ideology or deciphering mythologies to start questioning what is here being presented as 'natural' or 'normal' – namely, the 'heartbreak across the world'. It is sufficient to imagine people in other corners of the world, for instance parts of Africa that were under French colonial rule. Were they also 'heartbroken' while watching the images of the burning Notre-Dame? What about those millions of suffering people in Yemen: were they shocked in the same way as the Western spectators?

The Apocalypse is always a semiotic machine. Even if they represent different sorts of catastrophes, what both cases – flooded Venice and burning Notre-Dame – show is how disaster always takes places also in the semiosphere. What the narrative of such disasters reveals is both the ideology behind them and the material organization of our societies. Which brings us to the following question: what if the 'heartbreak across the world' and Venice's 'unique way of life' are nothing but monuments to our collective failure to create a sustainable reality beyond global capitalism, of which the global tourist industry is but one symptom? What if the historic centre of Venice, even if it still counts around 55,000 inhabitants (compared to the 180,000 in 1490 during the Republic of Venice), just like Dubrovnik and other tourist hot spots on both coasts of the Adriatic Sea, already is an empty ancient place 'frozen' in time, like a precious replica of itself reminding us of its previous 'unique way of life'? What if Venice is both dead and alive at the same time? And what if, in the end, it is nothing else but the death of Venice that is attracting, like a post-apocalyptic siren call, all those 22 million visitors every year? At least until the COVID-19 pandemic of 2020, which completely transformed global tourism and led to a significant decline in visitors.

What the process of 'normalization' covers up is not just the ideological core of 'caring for Venice' or 'caring for Notre-Dame', which is already grounded in a eurocentric classification of what is worth protecting and what is not worthy of 'heartbreak across the world'. What the floods in Venice reveal is that a 'natural disaster' is never just a 'natural disaster', at least when *Homo sapiens* is around; there is usually always something more than just the 'natural' in floods, hurricanes, drought and other current disasters. Yes, these are certainly events of nature, but their size and their effects are exacerbated by a specific economic system that turns disasters into something 'natural'. As the geographer Neil Smith put it back in 2006, writing about the devastating hurricane Katrina, 'in every phase and aspect of a disaster – causes, vulnerability, preparedness, results and response, and reconstruction – the contours of disaster and difference between who lives and who dies is to a greater or lesser extent a social calculus'.[46] It is this supposed 'naturalness' that 'becomes an ideological camouflage for the social (and therefore preventable) dimensions of such disasters, covering for quite specific social interests'.[47] In other words, it is a structural problem that underpins all these disasters (Katrina, Venice floods, not to mention the COVID-19 pandemic), which are often portrayed as 'natural'. And it is not just humans who are generating the catastrophe; it is being made possible by a particular system based on extraction and expansion. This led sociologist Jason Moore to propose the term 'Capitalocene', claiming that the Industrial Revolution that began in the nineteenth century is simply the consequence of a socioeconomic mutation that spawned capitalism in the 'long sixteenth century',[48] and that it is this world system – something that would become global capitalism, now turning into its authoritarian and techno-totalitarian version – that has led to geological changes, not humans themselves.[49] Only after global capitalism occupied the whole planet with its logic of 'growth', extraction and expansion, did humans become the 'masters of the Apocalypse'.

Even before the term 'Capitalocene' was coined, Félix Guattari, in his book *The Three Ecologies*, published in 1989 – incidentally or not, the same year that Francis Fukuyama published his notorious proclamation of the 'End of History' – argued that the ecological crisis that threatens our planet is a direct result of the expansion of a new form of capitalism and proposed a sort of 'mental ecology' that 'must stop being associated with the image of small nature-loving minority or with qualified specialists'.[50] Ecophilosophy, in Guattari's sense, 'questions the whole of subjectivity and capitalistic power formations, whose sweeping progress cannot be guaranteed to continue as it has for the past decade'.[51]

In other words, it is global capitalism that is killing Venice and the Mediterranean, not humans themselves. And this was, indeed, already visible even before the floods came. In the times before the COVID-19 pandemic, numerous coastal cities in Italy and Croatia were already becoming open-air museums flooded by hordes of tourists during summers, and ghostly empty during winter months. Every apartment in their historic centres was available for rent (usually via Silicon Valley companies like Airbnb), every corner had been turned into a cafe or a restaurant for tourists, everything was organized around tourism, and the service and gig economy. Flights across and above the Mediterranean contributing to climate change, the oil burned by cruisers and numerous ferries during the summer seasons, the sailing boats ruining the sea floor with their anchors and disposal of plastic garbage: all this was not so much a result of the 'Anthropocene' but rather of the 'Capitalocene'. It's not humans as such, but global capitalism that is catapulting us into disaster. And as long as capital (all those ships, containers, products) and humans (tourists, not refugees) can circulate, everything appears 'normal' – or, more precisely, as long as the pathology (extraction, expansion and exploitation) is normalized, capitalism can continue digging its own grave. The difference today is that capitalism is not simply digging its own grave; it is digging the grave for our planet as well, leading to total destruction.

And it is, again, the Mediterranean where you can detect that the Capitalocene will make a profit even out of its own funeral. In the good old days, it was Pompeii, but soon every city on both sides of the Adriatic coast was turned into a postmodern Pompeii. If the accumulation of capital is based on extractivism (just take the extraction of natural resources or the extraction of human labour), why wouldn't capitalism also extract the symbolic, semiotic or historic value of certain places like Venice through means of 'vampire-like' global tourism that is only living by sucking the 'living currency', namely the production of desire?[52] And even further: what if such post-apocalyptic images actually provoke a sort of dark apocalyptic desire (perhaps *Todestrieb* or even *jouissance*), or at least a 'phantasy of the end' that comes into being when such events occur?

In his renowned letter exchange with Cardinal Martini from Milan that took place between 1995 and 1996, the Italian novelist and semiotician Umberto Eco described this as a 'secular obsession with the new Apocalypse', saying that 'each one of us flirts with the specter of the apocalypse, exorcising it; the more one unconsciously fears it the more one exorcises, projecting it onto the screen in the form of bloody spectacle, hoping in this way to render it unreal'. 'But the power of specter', warns Eco, 'lies precisely in its unreality.'[53] And where was the secular obsession with the new Apocalypse anywhere more clear than in Venice after the floods of November 2019?

Just before the COVID-19 pandemic was to break out and turn numerous Italian cities into 'ghost towns', the spectre of the 'Death of Venice' was already haunting the popular imagination and the power of this spectre, as Eco would say, lay precisely in its 'unreality'. As the popular St Mark's Square was submerged under water, with the thousand-year-old St Mark's Basilica flooded for only the second time in a century, the dirty and corrosive water was penetrating the marble tombs inside the twelfth-century crypt. Luca Zaia, governor of the Veneto region, described a scene of 'apocalyptic devastation',[54] while Mario Piana, who heads the restoration of the damaged ancient marble floors of the Basilica, compared it to nothing less than *radioactivity*. 'The Basilica looks intact,' explained Piana, 'but this was not a flood like the one in Florence, which washes everything away and wreaks destruction. St Mark's is like a patient exposed to radiation: on the first day, nothing seems to have happened; then, a little later, their teeth and hair start falling out.'[55] The equivalent of radiation here is salt water, which is gradually causing the stone of the columns to crumble: 'If you take an X-ray, it might seem a minor problem. But if you're exposed to Chernobyl – and these repeated floods are like one Chernobyl after another – the accumulated damage is enormous. St Mark's apocalypse has already begun.'[56]

Even if this description represents another recent illustration of the 'secular obsession with the new Apocalypse', there is, indeed, a small step from the winds of the Mediterranean to the winds of Chernobyl, from floods to radioactivity, namely, from climate crisis to the nuclear age. You can take a ferry from Split to the island of Vis and the very next moment you are in the midst of a storm that makes your return impossible. For those of us who experienced that *sirocco* blowing over our heads and have seen the Adriatic coasts and islands swallowed by exceptionally large waves, the Mediterranean looked as if the Apocalypse had already happened – namely, as the 'revelation' of things to come. It was a short glimpse into the future of the ultimate flood described by Noah in Günther Anders's prophetic story. Little did we know at that moment that all the Adriatic islands and cities would soon, only a few months later, become 'excluded zones' – not because of the wind or radioactivity, but because of a virus. And, even before we know it, we are back to the future Mediterranean that perhaps only a year earlier would have been dismissed as science fiction or a mad prophecy by poor Noah who came to warn us that we have to mourn tomorrow's dead – including the death of the Mediterranean – today. Because the day after tomorrow it will be too late.

2

The Nuclear Age: 'Enjoy Chernobyl, Die Later'

This wasn't an ordinary fire, it was some kind of emanation. It was pretty. I'd never seen anything like it in the movies. That evening everyone spilled out onto their balconies, and those who didn't have them went to friend's houses. We were on the ninth floor, we had a great view. People brought their kids out, picked them up, said, 'Look! Remember!' They stood in the black dust, talking, breathing, wondering at it. People came from all around on their cars and their bikes to have a look. We didn't know that death could be so beautiful.'
Svetlana Alexievich, *The Voices from Chernobyl*, 1997

'Cloud that stopped at the border'

In September 2019, I received an automatic email reply from the tourist agency called CHERNOBYL TOUR with the subject 'Successfully booked #2012-4931'. It confirmed that the booking for my trip to the notorious 'Exclusion Zone' later that year was paid for, and informed me to read ten points of their message really carefully.

The first among them was the exact address of the meeting point in Kyiv, near the Central Railway Station. I was instructed that the buses would have a logo of the tourist company and would leave at exactly 8:00 a.m. The next point was that it's obligatory to have your passport with you, because it's impossible to enter the Zone without a passport, at least if you are a tourist – stalkers do their own thing (but the tourist agency didn't mention that yet). It's necessary to wear long sleeves (jacket, shirt), trousers, closed comfortable shoes and a hat, because of the weather conditions. It is PROHIBITED to wear any open type of clothing or footwear in the Zone. Then, as an early sign of the 'normalization' of the Apocalypse, it informed me that it is possible to pre-book a vegetarian dish if I wished to have lunch at the socialist cantina of the Chernobyl Nuclear Plant. And that it's possible to rent or buy a dosimeter for the short touristic stay in the 'Exclusion Zone'.

As I was reading these and other instruction points from the 'manual for survival' in Chernobyl more than three decades after the nuclear meltdown, it was impossible not to recall where I had been in 1986 as the radioactive cloud was drifting over Europe in the week after the accident. Each of us has a personal history of catastrophes and a subjective relation to it that is always lurking – usually in the unconscious – beneath the so-called 'normality' of daily life. My experience of Chernobyl was neither spectacular nor tragic. I happened to be a 3-year-old kid living with my parents in Munich, Germany. Little did I know what was happening, except that the parks were closed, but for a child of such a young age, it was probably difficult to comprehend why the parks, now that it was spring, were closed all over Bavaria. Little did I know that a dangerous threat could be invisible. And it is in the region of my childhood, Bavaria, as I would find out only much later, that the highest level of fallout fell in all Germany. Did I as a child, together with my parents, like all Germans, watch that iconic TV news on ARD, *Tagesschau*, on 29 April 1986, with a TV presenter in front of a map of Russia, Ukraine, Scandinavia and parts of Western Europe, speaking about the radio-active cloud that, according to the German officials, was not dangerous at all?

How did the population in Germany feel in 1986 when the minister of interior Friedrich Zimmermann (CSU) told the *Tagesschau*, three days after the catastrophe, that any concerns about danger can be 'absolutely excluded': 'Because there is only danger within a radius of 30 to 50 kilometres around the reactor, and we are 2,000 kilometres away.'[1] Wolfang Schäuble, who would later become the notorious German finance minister responsible for imposing austerity across the Eurozone, was also saying, on another TV channel (NRD), that there was no danger.[2] But just like the politicians who more often than not change direction, so too does the wind. And, as we would soon see in Germany, so do the radioactive clouds that couldn't care less what the politicians say.

And once again we are back to the importance of the wind, only we are not in the Mediterranean anymore and this time the clouds are radioactive. In 1986, after the Chernobyl disaster, the wind blew first towards the north, bringing the fallout to Poland, then to Sweden and Finland, but within only two days, as the German authorities were still comforting and deceiving the public into believing that there was no danger at all, it headed towards Czechoslovakia, finally reaching Austria, eastern parts of Germany and Yugoslavia. Munich was 1,800 kilometres away from Chernobyl – but radioactivity, unlike politicians who insist on borders, is obviously unaware of such things. The clouds didn't really care whether they were East or West of the

Iron Curtain, whether they were over this or that nation-state, this or that culture, this or that ideology, whether it's real existing socialism or real existing capitalism.

Suddenly, as the children of Bavaria couldn't grasp why it was prohibited to play in public parks and sandboxes, their parents were watching a frightening science fiction movie that appeared real on the TV, but 'unreal' in reality. At the beginning of May 1986, Western German news programmes, at least, were starting to show dystopian images of cows prohibited from grazing on fields, and cars being checked for radio-activity at the German borders (Eastern TV channels were still calling it just an 'incident'). In Stuttgart's supermarkets, fresh vegetables like salads, spinach and parsley were banned; in Wiesbaden, kids stood in front of a playground with a warning sign saying DO NOT ENTER; Munich closed its 'Freibad' (public swimming pool), which had only just reopened; in Stanberg, firefighters were on the streets cleaning all public spaces and schools. People were in a panic, but if you were to go to the streets of Munich, even though they were quite empty for late April, this all felt somewhat 'unreal'.[3] You couldn't see radioactivity. The threat was invisible. But as the rain poured down over Bavaria four days after the Chernobyl reactor exploded, the danger would become visible in its effects. Munich became a city of ghosts. Until life went back to 'normal'. But even 33 years later, measurements show that there are still radioactive mushrooms and boars in Bavaria that contain high levels of caesium-137.[4]

As I was thinking about my parents in 1986, and how they reacted to all this as a family that had just faced a personal 'apocalypse' and emigrated to Germany from Yugoslavia only three years earlier, I suddenly remembered Günther Anders again. Where was the philosopher of the nuclear age at that time? What happened when life turned to 'normal', after the Apocalypse, for instance – one month later? In late May 1986, when I was still a 3-year-old kid from Yugoslavia, probably playing again in the Munich playgrounds with my sister and my Turkish friends, and as children of Pripyat were finally evacuated from the 'Exclusion Zone', Günther Anders was 84 years old, travelling from Vienna to Cologne. More than 1,500 physicians from 65 countries were also travelling to Cologne, to attend the Sixth World Congress of the International Physicians for the Prevention of Nuclear War to examine the ethical aspects and existential threat posed by nuclear energy.[5]

A few weeks earlier, French TV was still reporting on the 'cloud that stopped at the border' (*le nuage qui s'est arrêté à la frontière*),[6] something that wasn't just ignorance but 'fake news' *avant la lettre* (which certainly wasn't an invention of Donald Trump or the twenty-first century) – as if radioactive clouds care about the French Republic and its laws and borders. In this kind of denialist atmosphere and blindness towards the catastrophe, Günther Anders addressed the physicians and scientists of the world, the 'contemporaries of the end times', with a powerful speech titled 'Ten theses on Chernobyl'. An historic speech that is becoming even more relevant today with the proliferation of nuclear weapons and nuclear energy.

One of the main points of Anders's speech was that the real danger consists in its *invisibility*.[7] Not just because radioactivity is invisible, but because the understanding of the complexity of this eschatological threat is beyond our psychological and neural capacity. It is literally too big to grasp. Those who have warned about this threat, says Anders, as if he had already predicted what kind of reaction would await Greta Thunberg and the children's climate movement in 2019, have been accused of 'sowing panic' and of being 'emotional' and 'irrational'.

Nevertheless, warns Anders, it is our duty to make a profession of 'sowing panic', because the real danger is not in the panic but in the danger against which this panic is addressed. And it should be shameful not to react in any other way but emotional. Because what is at stake is what Anders calls 'globocide', the destruction of the terraqueous globe.

As the Chernobyl reactor was still burning, he warned that the supporters of nuclear energy are no better than President Truman, who ordered the bombing of Hiroshima. Why? Because, for Anders, 'to distinguish between the military use and peaceful use of nuclear energy is senseless and deceitful', while 'peaceful nuclear power plants are instead nothing but a continuation of the military threat by way of the intervention of other means ... : today's peace is nothing but the continuation of war by other means.'[8]

Against the narrative of a threat that was not communicated as such, not only by the Soviet regime, but also by most of Europe's politicians and Western media who reported 'the cloud that stopped at the border', to proclaim that 'Chernobyl is everywhere' certainly came as a cold shower in the age of dogmatic slumber, or what Anders – decades before the Chernobyl explosion had occurred – called 'apocalyptic blindness' (*Apokalypse-Blindheit*).[9] We are 'blind' towards the Apocalypse because we don't have the ability to understand the scope and scale of the eschatological threat opened up by the nuclear age. What Anders was referring to with his dictum 'Chernobyl is everywhere' wasn't just the obvious fact that radioactivity, due to weather conditions, can cross 2,000 kilometres and reach previously unthreatened places. Chernobyl was everywhere not only as a *place*, but as *time* – it is temporality itself that is affected by the nuclear age.

In 1957, in what has to be considered one of his classic essays 'Commandments in the atomic age',

Anders warns us to widen our sense of time, noting that 'it is not only that the space of our Planet has shrunk together, that all places have become interconnected and neighbouring points, but also that the points in the system of our *time* have been drawn together'.[10] And where could we have seen it more clearly (even if we didn't really see it and we were 'blind' towards the disaster) but in Europe in 1986, 'that the futures which only yesterday had been considered unreachably far away, have now become neighbouring regions of our present time: that we have made them into "neighbouring communities"'.[11]

One month after Chernobyl, during his speech in Cologne, Anders returns to his previous 'commandments' and not only reformulates his dictum 'Hiroshima is everywhere' into 'Chernobyl is everywhere', but also warns that the whole Earth could be transformed into something much worse than Hiroshima: 'Because not only all locations in space, but also all points in time will be affected, if they have not already been affected. Then we, the men of our time and also our ancestors, will finally never have existed.'[12]

Incidentally, this is also how Svetlana Alexievich, the Belarus investigative journalist and oral historian who was awarded the 2015 Nobel Prize in Literature, formulated the temporal catastrophe that happened with Chernobyl:

I see Chernobyl as the beginning of a new history ... because it challenges our old ideas about ourselves and the world. When we talk about the past or the future, we read our ideas about time into those words; but Chernobyl is, above all, a catastrophe of time ... . In the space of one night we shifted to another place in history ... beyond not only our knowledge but also our imagination. Time was out of joint. The past suddenly became impotent, it had nothing for us to draw on; in the all-encompassing – or so we'd believed – archive of humanity, we couldn't find a key to open this door ... . We now find ourselves on a new page of history. The history of disasters has begun ... But people do not want to reflect on that ... preferring to take refuge in the familiar.[13]

How strange and frightening that French TV news reportage must have looked, which even showed a traffic 'STOP' sign at the border (to visualize that the 'cloud stopped at the border'), to all those people who had been evacuated from Pripyat and the surrounding area of the Chernobyl disaster. How illusionary it looks today when the effects of radioactivity didn't surpass just borders, but also time, leading to cancer and death. This STOP sign at the beginning of an epoch that would be proclaimed as the 'end of history' was the pure embodiment of the illusion that what surrounds us is a stable world in which such concepts as national borders or even sovereignty, when faced with the planetary disaster, still play a significant role. Even the 'Exclusion Zone' itself, as the historian Kate Brown notes in her important book *Manual for Survival. A Chernobyl Guide to the Future*, 'was just a circle drawn on a map. It didn't stop radiation from transgressing its borders'.[14]

The world is unstable, and it will never be stable again, because the eschatological threat today is 'supraliminal' (*überschwellig*): it exceeds the ordinary human experience and capacity to understand. While the psychologist Gustav T. Fechner introduced the idea of stimuli that are so weak that they are 'subliminal' and remain below the threshold of our perception and consciousness (the way propaganda or 'manufacturing consent' works), Anders introduced the concept of the 'supraliminal' to describe a situation in which stimuli are *too strong* to be registered by our perception – or even our imagination.

The history of disasters has certainly begun (actually it never stopped), but it is not just that people do not want to reflect on it, it is more that we are unable to fully grasp this reality – it is beyond the limits *(supraliminal)* of our comprehension. That is why it is usually easier to take refuge in the familiar. Because the 'unfamiliar' (or Freud's *unheimlich*), even if we turn it into the 'sublime' (as it often happens as an exit strategy when we are confronted with extraordinary events), is way too strong to really confront. According to Anders, there is a gap between the Apocalypse (the 'revelation') and our capacity to understand it:

> The possibility of the Apocalypse is our work. But we know not what we are doing. We really don't know, nor do they who control the Apocalypse: for they too are 'we', they too are fundamentally incompetent. That they too are incompetent, is certainly not their fault; rather the consequence of a fact for which neither they nor we can be held responsible: the effect of the daily growing gap between our two faculties; between our *actions* and our *imagination*; of the fact, that we are unable to conceive what we can construct; to mentally reproduce what we can produce; to realize the reality which we can bring into being.[15]

Demonstrating how her work and thinking were intrinsically linked with that of Anders, how the same preoccupations (from totalitarianism and Auschwitz to the total annihilation of humanity) were chasing them and bringing them together after their escape from Nazi Germany, Hannah Arendt expressed the same kind of fear in the prologue of her book *The Human Condition*, written around the same time as Anders was writing his 'Commandments':

> We do not yet know whether this situation is final. But it could be that we, who are earth-bound creatures,

have begun to act as though we were dwellers of the universe, will forever be unable to understand, that is, to think and speak about the things which nevertheless we are able to do. In this case, it would be as though our brain, which constitutes the physical, material condition of our thoughts, was unable to follow what we do, so that from now on we would indeed need artificial machines to do our thinking and speaking. If it should turn out to be true that knowledge (in the modern sense of know-how) and thought have parted company for good, then we would indeed become helpless slaves, not so much of our machines as of our know-how, thoughtless creatures at the mercy of every gadget which is technically possible, no matter how murderous it is.[16]

This was written decades before Chernobyl. But it is as if both Anders, in qualifying those 'who control the Apocalypse' as 'fundamentally incompetent', and Arendt, by describing 'our brain' as unable to 'follow what we do', were already sensing Chernobyl (a result of a fundamentally incompetent bureaucracy of the late Soviet Union) and also what would come later, namely, Fukushima (which was, again, not just a mere 'natural' catastrophe). This gap between our *actions* and our *imagination*, which would turn us into 'thoughtless creatures at the mercy of every gadget', was called by Anders 'the Promethean gap' (*Das Prometheische Gefälle*) – the profound gap between our technical ability to create (like the nuclear bomb or climate change) and our (in)capacity to fully understand the actual effects of this creation.[17]

Today when Chernobyl already looks like a footnote to a much bigger world catastrophe (or even globocide), this gap is not only growing but turning into an abyss.

The obsolescence of 'ruin value'

Nowhere is the Apocalypse as 'revelation' about an end of a 'world' so intense as in places that have already been turned into ruins. Because these places were always much more than just 'places' consisting of buildings and architecture, they were 'worlds' that would soon vanish and become 'worldless'. And again, no one understood it better than Günther Anders, whose whole œuvre could be understood as a philosophy that was coming to terms with ruins. While he was still in exile in New York in 1943, looking at a picture of an *'ausgebrannten Stadt'* (burned-out city) in Europe, Anders notes in his diaries (posthumously published in Germany):

> How ridiculous at the sight of such a ruin the alternative-distinction between person and thing [appears]! Is it really so self-evident that the death of one man is an absolutely greater loss than that of a city? That [the death] of Archimedes is greater than the [death of] Syracuse? Is a city a 'thing' at all? Isn't it a 'world' that makes the 'people' living in it (what an embarrassing abstract word for the Viennese or Berliner) into what they are, urbanized in this way and no other? Won't the residents, even if they saved their bare lives, now that their city is ruined, also be ruined? – If Paris perished, wouldn't it be the end of the world?[18]

Two years later, still in New York, he couldn't stop thinking of Europe and its devastated cities and worlds, noting how at least one of these ruins should be preserved as a monument to the catastrophe, so that everyone, every single day, could see what had been done, who had done it – and so that it would never be forgotten.[19] A year later, he is looking at a picture of the ruins of the *Kaiser-Wilhelm Gedächtniskirche* in Berlin and notes in his diary: 'One should not build monuments, but adopt things as monuments. For instance, the ruins of this church. As a monument to Hitler.'[20] And, indeed, the church nicknamed by Berliners *'der hohle Zahn'* (meaning 'the hollow tooth') is a famous landmark and monument of western Berlin today. Reading Anders's philosophical diaries, we can at the same time read how his view on the 'theory of ruins' gradually changed from considering the ruins as something that were better preserved than forgotten, to a deeper understanding of the relation between places and people, between past and future, between destruction and the impossibility of salvation.

Then, a few years later, in rediscovering post-war Europe, Anders travels by train to Cologne from where, as the train was entering the city on the Rhine, he could already see the first ruins of the place that had been

Figure 4: Cologne in ruins after Allied bombings, 1944

one of the most heavily bombarded cities in Germany during the Second World War, with the RAF dropping more than 30,000 tons of bombs on the city. And it is here, perhaps after seeing the image of the still standing cathedral that seemed to have survived only to mark the destruction of the surrounding area, that Anders finally admits how 'hopelessly illusionary' his previous 'hope' about a 'ruin monument' was: 'The ruins are preserved; even today, after so many years. But who cares about them? To whom are they monuments and for what? And who should they be reminding tomorrow if there is no one left already today who sees them as monuments?'[21]

Then finally, one evening in June 1953, he is back at the *Gedächtniskirche* in Berlin, the photograph of which he saw during his American exile, and, while standing in front of the church waiting for someone to look up at it (but that person never arrives), he finally comes to a conclusion about the value of ruins: 'Nobody thinks of Hitler more than of Kaiser Wilhelm the First, to whose memory the church was once built.'[22] It was here that the notorious Nazi theory of 'ruin value' (*Ruinenwert*) was pulled to pieces.

The idea that even the ruins would become a monument to Hitler was pioneered by the notorious German architect, and later Reich Minister for Armaments and War Production, Albert Speer (1905–81). Already in early 1934 he was commissioned by Adolf Hitler himself – who just like Benito Mussolini glorified ancient Roman monuments and understood the power of architecture – to build a structure inspired by the ancient Pergamon Altar at the *Zeppelinfeld* for the big Nazi party rallies. Here he would develop the *Ruinenwert* ('ruin value') that would soon become one of Hitler's favourite concepts, not only as a way of using architecture and urbanism in order to show the greatness of the Millennial Reich, but actually foreseeing the future ruins that would symbolize the greatness of the Third Reich, even after the demise of the empire.

To illustrate his ideas, as if he was preparing a set for a post-apocalyptic TV series like *Chernobyl*, Speer showed Hitler a science fiction drawing that depicted the Zeppelin Field after the *Götterdämmerung* – or 'after the Apocalypse' – overgrown with ivy and with its column fallen, but with still recognizable outlines. As Speer recalls, in Hitler's circle this drawing was regarded as blasphemous – that he could even conceive of a period of decline for the just founded Third Reich destined to last at least a thousand years. But unlike his closest and outraged followers, Hitler actually liked the idea and even gave orders that, in the future, all the important buildings of the Reich were to be erected following the principles of this 'law of ruins'.[23]

Even if he claimed to have invented the idea, Albert Speer was certainly not the first one to understand the 'value of ruins'; it can be traced back to the Romantic fascination with ruins that would reach its peak with the fascination with Pompeii. In his memoirs *Inside the Third Reich*, he recalled how Adolf Hitler himself understood this 'law':

> Hitler liked to say that the purpose of his building was to transmit his time and its spirit to posterity. Ultimately, all that remained to remind men of the great epochs of history was their monumental architecture, he would philosophize. What had remained of the emperors of Rome? What would still bear witness to them today, if their buildings had not survived? Periods of weakness are bound to occur in history of nations, he argued: but at their lowest ebb, their architecture will speak to them of former power.[24]

And here we come back to Günther Anders, a victim of Hitler's fascination with the ruins who had to find refuge in the United States in order to escape the Nazi regime, and his travels throughout post-apocalyptic Europe after the Second World War. Did the 'law of ruins' really work and leave such an impression on those whose lives, precisely thanks to Hitler and Mussolini, were turned into ruins? And why would anyone, in the first place, still be fascinated by ruins? When in 1958 Anders finally visited Rome, he just couldn't handle it anymore. He was literally fed up with ruins:

> But my eyes, they don't want to take part in this anymore. They can't anymore. They don't want anymore. Not because they were too old or too weak, but because they have seen things that are too strong. In the times of real ruins, to think of ruins as beautiful, that goes beyond the power [of the eyes]. And beyond their time. And beyond their taste. And already the day after tomorrow – I am convinced – there will be only a few left who will find that what is destroyed beautiful because it is destroyed.[25]

A few years later, in December 1962, he is back to the *urbs aeterna* (the 'eternal city'), and notes in his diary that he knows of no other city that 'hammered into us the continuity of mortality as relentlessly and at every turn as this collection of ruins. What a self-deception to see something eternal in these [ruins] just because they are still there.'[26] After the 'eternal city', as if these ruins were not enough for his eyes, Anders visited the legendary ancient Pompeii where he couldn't get rid of an 'irritable' feeling of *déjà vu*. Where did this happen? 'And suddenly', he recalls, 'I saw myself wandering through Cologne, between bombed buildings right and left. That could have looked exactly like here [in Pompeii]. Whether something died yesterday or nineteen hundred years ago – the effect is the same: what is left over, namely the ruin, immediately has a "timeless" effect.'[27]

As he was wandering through Pompeii, Anders realized the following paradox: the reason why this place is preserved was precisely the catastrophe that ruined it, while other cities from ancient times didn't survive simply because they still live – a better example than Rome is certainly Naples about whose 'porosity' Walter Benjamin and Asja Lacis were already writing.[28] And isn't this still true today? When you go to a place such as Naples or Rome, you can see the ruins or archaeological sites within the modern cities; life goes on after someone's 'end of the world'. On the other hand, when you go inside the city walls of ancient Pompeii, there isn't anything (except the tourists) that isn't Roman – here, the 'end of the world' is frozen. And it is precisely thanks to the catastrophe that this is possible: the eruption of Vesuvius in 79 CE both destroyed and preserved the relatively insignificant town of Pompeii and turned its ruins into an object of fascination. Destruction, in this case, was preservation. And it even added an additional value to it and provoked an everlasting fascination and phantasy with its 'frozen' end.

Once it was 'rediscovered' in the early eighteenth century, Pompeii would fit perfectly into the prevailing apocalyptic discourse in the aftermath of the great earthquake at Lisbon in 1755 and the dramatic eruptions of Vesuvius in the late 1770s. It became part of the apocalyptic imaginary that would take various forms, from novels and movies (from Edward Bulwer-Lytton's bestseller novel *The Last Days of Pompeii* to Roberto Rossellini's film *Journey to Italy*), to paintings and operas, and even 'dark tourism' might perhaps have found its origin precisely in the 'City of the Dead'.

At the beginning, this sort of exclusive tourism was, as always, reserved for the rich. The best example is the notorious *Gabinetto Segreto* (The Secret Museum), constructed in 1795 to display erotic frescoes and sexually explicit content that were considered 'pornography' during the nineteenth century. The door was still bricked up in 1848, while later it would be accessible only to 'people of mature age and respected morals'; it was then closed again for nearly 100 years, and has been open to the public only since 2000. At that time, when Pompeii had already become a tourist spot for the rich, the 'secret cabinet' was reserved for the aristocracy.

That the modern version of 'dark tourism' might have originated in Pompeii is best to be seen in an old article entitled 'Pompeii by Torch-light' published in 1835, describing a nocturnal journey through the excavations by a Bavarian prince, 'whose nobility affords the opportunity to explore the ruins unaccompanied by guides' and avoid stumbling upon the 'gawky curiosity' of common tourists.[29] Instead, privileged tourists could visit the preserved houses and artefacts of the 'Dead City' and experience the Apocalypse, this 'worldless' world which is both dead and alive at the same time. Then, later in the eighteenth century, both Pompeii and Herculaneum became regular spots for the upper-class young Europeans and Americans on their 'Grand Tour', and it would slowly enter the popular imagination through postcards and photographs, including the plaster casts (*gessi*) by Giuseppe Fiorelli, those un-dead people and dogs whose death was 'frozen' in time.

It is exactly this 'timelessness' that attracts us so much to the ruins. Pompeii wasn't just a paradise for archaeologists and psychoanalysts (take Sigmund Freud's exploration of the 'return of the repressed' through the ghostly figure of Gradiva),[30] it is a paradise for urbanists and architects, but also political scientists and anyone who wants to understand society. What the ruins of Pompeii reveal or 'unveil' are not only internal links between different ancient institutions, like the temples of Jupiter or Apollo or the Basilica ('palace of justice'), shops and restaurants (*tavernas*), pedestrian streets and political graffiti; they also reveal the dining preferences of the inhabitants, their political economy, sexual and political practises, libidinal investments and desires. The carbonized food of both the wealthy and their slaves reveals not only the habits of the Roman people; at the same time, it points towards the class differences and political constitution of that society. It is a mirror to our own societies and what we do differently – or, rather, the same.

Although it seems that Pompeii succeeded in 'surviving' the end of a world, even if only as a 'frozen' image of the past, just before the COVID-19 pandemic it was questionable whether it would be able to survive the record-breaking annual tourist visits. As the *New York Times* showed in an article titled 'Can a restored Pompeii be saved from "clambering" tourists?', in 2009 nearly 2.1 million people visited the site. By 2018, that figure had risen to more than 3.6 million, an increase of more than 70 per cent. In 2019, nearly 450,000 people visited Pompeii in July alone, marking the highest monthly figure ever recorded.[31] Compared to about 12,000 people who lived in the ancient Roman town throughout the year, this is a significant influx of people and an existential threat for the 'frozen' Pompeii. Yet, whatever happens to Pompeii as a result of global tourism, this post-apocalyptic place has obviously been used to the fatal repetition of the end. In fact, the fatal eruption of Vesuvius 79 CE was just one of the eruptions preceded by others in prehistory, including three significantly larger ones – for instance, the powerful Avellino eruption two millennia before Pompeii.

Post-apocalyptic places such as Pompeii, which was a relatively minor seaside town largely dedicated to serving villas and a culture of '*otium*' (leisure), serve not only as a unique window into the 'frozen past', they offer at the same time a glimpse into one of our possible futures. And here we must undertake a temporal – not just geographical – jump to another place, namely to the Pompeii of the nuclear age, carrying with us the following question: what if our contemporary ruins are much more sinister than the ones left by the eruption of Vesuvius?

Officially, post-apocalyptic tourism to Chernobyl had already started in 2011, on the 25th anniversary of the disaster, when Ukraine announced that the 'Exclusion Zone' would be open to tourists. Back then, newspapers were writing about a new era of tourism: 'Already been to North Korea? Hiking in Afghanistan a little bit too last year? Fear not. Tourism has a new frontier: the site of the world's biggest civilian nuclear disaster.'[32] This was even before the new sarcophagus for the exploded reactor had been completed. And at the time when the old sarcophagus was still leaking radiation, Chernobyl was already turning into a site of so-called 'dark tourism', a place of disaster that was becoming commodified and consumed as a tourist experience.

In 2017, after two decades of design and construction, Chernobyl's 'New Safe Confinement' finally became operational. This €1.5 billion structure aims to contain the spread of radioactive debris, while workers inside dismantle the reactor and its crumbling previous sarcophagus. At the transfer ceremony, newly elected Ukrainian President Volodymyr Zelensky announced a tourism development plan for the radioactive exclusion zone, including a 'green corridor' through which tourists could travel to gaze at the remains of Soviet hubris.[33]

'Until now, Chernobyl was a negative part of Ukraine's brand,' declared Zelensky, who was 9 years old when the reactor exploded. 'It's time to change.'[34] And the times have changed, indeed. Instead of arriving at Fukuyama's 'end of history', we reached the 'End-Time' (*die Endzeit*), and furthermore we are living in times in which apparently even the Apocalypse could become a tourist attraction. What Günther Anders, this great philosopher of ruins who was convinced that 'ruin value' was obsolete, probably didn't expect was something that we might call the 'commodification of the Apocalypse'.

Commodification of the Apocalypse

On 25 October 2019, while I happened to be in Jihlava, around 1,000 kilometres from Chernobyl and some 60 kilometres from the Czech nuclear power plant Dukovany, my inbox suddenly received an email with the subject 'Reminder about the CHERNOBYL TOUR'. It reminded me, as tourist agencies usually do, that the date for my trip to the 'Exclusion Zone' was 29 October 2019. A few days later, when I finally arrived at Kyiv, I was, indeed, a tourist in search of the post-apocalypse. Like so many others who came to explore the nuclear Pompeii.

When you are a tourist going for a pre-arranged tourist trip, especially when it is a visit to a post-apocalyptic place, what makes this position 'special' (at least as a position from which to detect and read ideology) is precisely that there is seemingly nothing 'special' in it – that almost everything is already pre-arranged and mediated. What interested me wasn't so much the 'authentic' experience – with the legendary 'stalkers' you would certainly get a deeper understanding and 'better' experience of the place (even though you would still be a 'tourist'). What interested me in this sort of 'field philosophy' was precisely the opposite: to experience what thousands of people want to experience, to understand what 'post-apocalyptic tourism' is all about and why is it becoming so popular in the twenty-first century. Or at least, why it was so popular until the outbreak of the COVID-19 pandemic when global tourism came to a halt.

I would soon find out, even before reaching Chernobyl. As I was walking down the Symona Petlyury Street towards Kyiv's central railway station, there were already three mini-buses (each could comfortably fit 15–20 people) parked on the road with 'Chernobyl' signs. One of the drivers approached me asking 'Are you going to Chernobyl?' But I remembered the instructions telling me I would have to pass the railway station towards the south and exit the Yuzhniy terminal to reach the bus. Once I arrived at that location, four mini-buses were already ready to storm the nuclear palace of Chernobyl, with guides awaiting passengers from across the world. I handed over my passport for the guide to quickly track down the details, signed a paper that is required by the Ukranian government, and received a 'certificate' from the tourist agency, basically a printed map of the 'Exclusion Zone' with an empty box for the guide to fill out the level of radioactivity I would have received during that day until the return to Kyiv.

Once everyone was seated and the mini-bus had started its journey towards the border with Belarus and about 110 kilometres (70 miles) north of Kyiv, we were presented with a 'radiation safety' crash course at 8:00 a.m. in the morning. After a short introduction into the universe of the atom, the guide warned us that no animals, no drones, no drugs and no alcohol is permitted into the 'Exclusion Zone' – apparently the tours were becoming so popular in 2019 that some tourists would arrive in the morning directly from a crazy night out in Kyiv. Some would enter buildings, which is now prohibited by the Ukrainian government due to a fear that some of them might collapse, but also because of higher radioactivity that it is still possible to encounter there. In short, everything would be just fine – we were assured – if we follow the simple rules of our guide.

Then, while driving to the north of Ukraine, a movie

was shown on the TV screen in the mini-bus. It was called 'The Battle of Chernobyl'. We can see a machine operator who worked at the Reactor 4 describing the bright colours coming out of the explosion. 'Colours like blood, a rainbow. It was ... beautiful.' It reminded me of another description by another eye-witness recorded by Svetlana Alexievich: 'The image is still burned into my eyes: a bright crimson glow, the reactor somehow glowing from inside. It was an incredible colour. It wasn't an ordinary fire – it was like some kind of fluorescence. It was pretty.'[35]

While the tourist mini-bus was heading towards the 'Exclusion Zone', the short movie showed images of the nuclear disaster, the 'liquidators', Mikhail Gorbachev, and as soon as the movie was finished, the guide, a young Ukrainian who had been working for the tourist agency for three years, turned to us, the passengers, and asked who had watched the HBO series *Chernobyl* that premiered in May 2019. Everyone in the mini-bus, including me, raised their hands. In October 2018, there were 9,083 visitors to the 'Exclusion Zone'. In October 2019, there were more than 17,000.[36] And I was one of them, taking part in this post-apocalyptic tourist adventure. According to the State Agency of Ukraine, the increase in traffic began in spring 2019 at the same time as the release of the HBO *Chernobyl* series, and more than 100,000 tourists visited the 'Exclusion Zone' in 2019 (compared to 8,000 tourists in 2013).[37] Then in spring 2020 came the COVID-19 pandemic and there were no further trips to Chernobyl. Flights and tours were not operating, the area became silent again. And anyway, who would travel to a post-apocalyptic place when all the places in the world had now become ghostly and empty like the 'Exclusion Zone'? Yet it is precisely this short moment of the peak of post-apocalyptic tourism in Chernobyl that carries some lessons for the world 'after the Apocalypse'.

While we were driving towards Chernobyl in late October 2019, I could see several CHERNOBYL TOUR billboards. The danger might have been invisible, but post-apocalyptic tourism was pretty visible on every corner. It would become even more so once we reached, after a two-hour ride and our guide's 'introduction' to Chernobyl, the control point and official entrance to the 'Exclusion Zone'. As we approached, it was rather quiet and almost empty. But once we reached the checkpoint, it was suddenly full of trucks and something like 10–15 mini-buses, operated by various tourist agencies, plus a few cars doing so-called 'private tours'. And again, as in the good old times of the rediscovery of Pompeii in the early eighteenth century and its 'dark tourism', those with more money experienced the 'Exclusion Zone' away from the 'gawky curiosity' of common tourists.

We were told that we were still the lucky ones, since it was winter, so the number of tourists was lower, and the architecture, the houses in the surrounding villages and the buildings in Pripyat were more visible than during spring or summer when they would disappear behind the trees and be submerged in nature. While our guide was checking the papers with the police, we, the post-apocalyptic mass tourists, had just enough time to check out the souvenirs, ranging from magnets, mugs glowing in the dark, dosimeter 'pencils', personal protection equipment, 'radioactive' ice-cream and $19 canisters of Pripyat air with 'the unforgettable smell of abandoned structures of the Soviet Union, the dampness of basements, mixed with the aroma of Pripyat roses' – and last, but not least, a red T-shirt saying *Enjoy Chernobyl, die later*.

Today there is a wide range of products that reflect or materialize our current post-apocalyptic *Zeitgeist* – and it's not just Chernobyl. Where there is a possibility for profit, not even the end of the world is an obstacle. Quite the opposite: even the end of the world can be turned into a commodity. For instance, in the autumn of 2019, the company behind *The Walking Dead* comic series, together with global liquor giant Diageo, owner of brands like Smirnoff and Johnnie Walker, launched a special edition of what they called 'Spirits of the Apocalypse'. According to the website: 'Set in an apocalyptic world, where the dead feed off the living, society has crumbled to the verge of extinction. There is no government, no stores, no mail delivery, no cable TV. But luckily, there is bourbon.'[38]

In Ukraine, a team of social entrepreneurs went a step further and actually made an artisan vodka produced from grain grown in the 'Exclusion Zone' around Chernobyl. They called it, of course, 'Atomik'.[39] And while the slogan advertising fresh vegetables from Dutch farmers just after the Chernobyl disaster was simply 'radiation-free',[40] signalling that the food was not contaminated, the vodka is advertised also as 'radiation-free' (at least according to the post-apocalyptic entrepreneurs), but it is the very fact that it *does come* from the contamination zone that raises the value of the product.

Even when it comes to such spheres as love or sex, there are products that play with the Apocalypse or use the signifier in order to sell the signified or the product. In October 2019, the famous dating service app Tinder launched its first entertainment content, called 'Swipe Night', an interactive adventure series in which viewers are forced to make dating choices on humanity's last night on Earth. At the time of its launch, newspapers were writing that 'Tinder wants users to find love in the Apocalypse'[41] and 'Tinder's video game will show you how prospective matches handle an apocalypse'.[42] If love was already commodified and commercialized, as if it was merely a product on the 'free market', why wouldn't the Apocalypse be commodified as well?

Then, for the youngsters, there are new LEGO toys,

inspired by the movie, the so-called *Apocalypseburg*. It is an apocalyptic wasteland town resembling the scene from the *Planet of the Apes* with Charlton Heston's astronaut character screaming on the beach next to the Statue of Liberty. While in the past children were supposed to play with 'police' and 'pirates', building castles or cities, spaceships or hospitals, today it is obviously the Apocalypse that is becoming a content of their play. If even LEGO, which was among the rare toys that still to some degree treated children as creators and not mere users, envisaged a post-apocalyptic setting as a precondition for play, what is the future that is being signalled by our contemporary toys? What are the future roles our children should learn now, so that they can fit better into society 'after the Apocalypse'?

Obviously, they have to get used to the idea of the 'end of the world'. If children are generally being prepared for the 'adult' universe by playing adult roles (soldier, policeman, nurse, princess, superhero and so on),[43] what the *Apocalypseburg* prepares them for is nothing more than the ultimate future role everyone will have to assume – namely, the role of those who will live after the Apocalypse. If by playing with soldiers and guns, for instance, children usually 'naturalize' something that is not natural and certainly not fun (namely, war), then isn't playing with the Apocalypse a form of normalizing the 'end of the world' itself, transforming it into something that has already happened? Is it so difficult to imagine that, in our 'End-Time', an 'adult' is drinking the 'Spirits of the Apocalypse' while the ideal child, instead of protesting against the 'adults' and their destruction of the world, will be playing with the *Apocalypseburg*?

And we don't have to imagine this kind of dystopian scene as something probable, because this trend of what we could call *'fröhliche Apokalpyse'*, borrowing a term Hermann Broch used to describe the decadence of the Austro-Hungarian monarchy, is already happening, and we could have seen it in many places in the world during recent years. It was sufficient to look at Australia in early 2020, when the demand for anti-pollution masks spiked because of the air pollution produced by the unprecedented bushfires. It led the *Guardian* to report on 'fashionable face masks', describing one of the masks that can be found on the market in Australia as 'a soft yet utilitarian aesthetic – like something you might find on the Starship Enterprise'.[44]

Even before the COVID-19 pandemic, as air pollution was getting worse, face masks were already becoming an 'accessory' worldwide. 'In China and India, lifestyle bloggers review them as they would a new nail polish shade or handbag',[45] while in the United States, after the wildfires of California, start-ups were competing to produce 'dystopian accessories'.[46] And, again, in case you wondered, there are also products for children. The range of colours available for face masks isn't just about creating a product that's 'fashionable', according to one company's CEO. She says that the old masks looked quite militaristic but 'by adding colour you can convince a five-year-old to wear a mask'.[47] This was written in January 2020, and soon it would become true all over the world, where parents could afford to buy fashionable – or any – face masks for their kids in order to protect them from COVID-19.

What we can see here is a case of the *commodification of the Apocalypse*. If nowadays everything can become a commodity (data, rainforests, water, air and even love), why wouldn't the Apocalypse itself become one? While the ancient *memento mori* ('remember that you will die') was not only a reminder that we are mortal and that everything is vanishing but also a warning to live and know how to die, 'the commodification of the Apocalypse' contains no warning: it serves rather as an instance of acceptance – or 'normalization'

– of the inevitable end without the subversive twist of the *memento mori* that necessarily provokes a shock. A shock like the ancient Egyptian custom, mentioned by Michel de Montaigne in his essay *That to study philosophy is to learn to die* (1580), when, during times of festivities, a skeleton would be brought out with people cheering 'Drink and be merry, for such shalt thou be wen thou art dead'.[48]

However, for Montaigne, deeply influenced by Stoic thought, this was not just a mere variation of *carpe diem* (as Horace writes on the death of Cleopatra in his Odes, I.37, *nunc est bibendum, nunc pede libero pulsanda* ...), on the contrary, the premeditation of death was the premeditation of freedom itself, there was still something liberating in knowing that death will come. But today, even extinction is being commodified, children are already playing at the 'end of the world', and very often there is no shock anymore, no meditation over death or something much more sinister, namely the 'globocide'.

The commodification process of late global capitalism transforms even the 'end of the world' into an object, a product that has to be consumed even if the world is becoming thoroughly 'worldless'. The consequence of post-apocalyptic tourism is very often the erasure of the *memento mori*, and, instead of Horace's 'Now is the time for drinking now the time for dancing footloose', today it becomes 'Now it's time for the Apocalypse, now the time for selfies'. We even travel to distant and not so distant post-apocalyptic places and turn them not just into a spectacle, but into a commodity that becomes a sort of *ersatz* experience for an experience that would otherwise be too difficult to endure.

Supraliminal radioactivity

As soon as our mini-bus left the busy checkpoint with its souvenir shops and post-apocalyptic goodies, the road became totally empty again and we reached the deserted collective farming village Zalissya, once inhabited by around 3,000 people and now immersed into the forest with its empty houses and the uncanny Palace of Culture, streets overgrown with trees, a ghostly children's playground, rusted personal objects, shoes, pots, school material and a calendar from 1986 in a place that used to be someone's world before it became 'worldless'.

It is already here at the first stop in the 'Exclusion Zone', as *unheimlich* as it is to encounter for the first time the ghostly absence of humans and a temporality that is literally 'out of joint', where the Apocalypse is 'commodified'. Namely, both the calendar from 1986 and the children's toys were already *mediated*: we could have seen them in previous photos from the

Figure 5: T-shirt being sold in the Chernobyl 'Exclusion Zone'

'Exclusion Zone'; we were actually – even if we were on the conscious level not aware of it – expecting them in order to prove that this was 'real'.

And as I would find out later in Koppachi village, before being mediated (through all the popular images of what we refer to as 'Chernobyl'), some of these objects were actually *staged*. Like the famous kindergarten in Koppachi that is now a regular stop-over for all the tourist buses operating in the 'Exclusion Zone'. First, because it is placed near the burial ground of mainly wooden houses that absorbed a vast amount of radio-activity, which polluted the soil and water with highly radioactive materials such as plutonium and caesium-137, so you can check out spots of higher radioactivity with your dosimeter. And second, precisely because the images from the kindergarten somehow look more 'real' than the invisible radioactivity outside (even if you can 'hear' it from your dosimeter). As I would find out by entering it, together with other post-apocalyptic tourists, these were the same images I had seen before: the dolls, the beds, the schoolbooks ... And it is here where we can see how important mediation and staging (or framing) is in 'seeing the Apocalypse'.

When we finally reached the ghost-town of Pripyat, once home to around 50,000 citizens, besides the *staged* objects (like a rusted medical device in front of the notorious hospital, books around the floors, gas masks on trees), the *mediation* would return even more clearly in the form of photographs that our guide would show us in front of the deserted buildings and overgrown streets. *Here* is the swimming pool. *This* is how it looked before the disaster. *Here* is the amusement park. *This* is what it looked like. *Here* is the stadium and the supermarket. *This* is what it looked like. And here is the famous Polissya hotel, which once housed delega-tions and guests visiting the Chernobyl Power Plant and which first became part of popular imagination through the video game *Call of Duty 4: Modern Warfare*, back in 2007.

While *here–this* was reverberating throughout my trip to the Pripyat, I was suddenly transposed to another place and time where I had seen this already. But it wasn't the 'Exclusion Zone'. It was Dubrovnik, Croatia. During the tourist seasons, at least before the COVID-19 pandemic, you could see numerous groups of tourists consisting of 30–50 people with a guide in front of them showing photos in front of buildings or streets. Once you came closer, you would usually see the guide pointing at the photograph from the famous TV series and saying 'This is King's Landing', or 'This is where Queen Cersei walked the "path of shame"'. Here, in October 2019, it was another HBO-series whose screenshots were illustrating not an imaginary world of *Game of Thrones*, but 'real' Pripyat before the disaster. It was commodification at its purest.

As the guide was showing us images of Pripyat *before* the disaster, the message from the red T-shirt that is being sold not only at the entrance to the 'Exclusion Zone' but also all over Kyiv, started to unveil itself. On the level of signs, which is to say on the semiotic level, 'Enjoy Chernobyl, die later' is not just a successful marketing trick that is, with its iconic designed letters in red and white, evoking the famous Coca-Cola design. At the same time, it can be read as another version of the famous *sots art* work by the Russian American artist Alexander Kosolapov called *Lenin Coca-Cola*, made in 1982, that would place the profile of Vladimir Lenin next to Coca-Cola's logo and the company's slogan ('it's the real thing') is signed: Lenin.

If there ever was a more surreal encounter between Soviet ideology and Western consumerism, even before *Perestroika* and *Glasnost*, then it was in this joint venture of Coca-Cola and Lenin both appealing to the 'real thing'. As a proof that it obviously was pointing towards some 'real thing', Kosolapov's Lenin Coca-Cola was not welcomed, either in the Soviet Union or the United States, for quite obvious reasons – it was perceived as an attack on both Soviet ideology and Western ideology.[49] But what was the 'real thing'?

It was the image – and the imaginary itself – that was the 'real', not so much the soft drink called Coca-Cola, but 'the way of life' represented by it. Or as Umberto Eco put it in his *Travels in Hyperreality*, 'the American imagination demands the real thing and, to attain it, must fabricate the absolute fake'.[50] The absolute fake in this case, namely the 'real thing' that is more real than the original, was the utopian liberal dream called 'the end of history', whether sold by Coca-Cola advertisements or by Francis Fukuyama himself, the idea that all ideologies would vanish after the final victory of 'liberal democracy' that was supposed to be the final stage of human civilization. After the collapse of the Soviet Union and after the proclaimed 'end of history', when both West and East were happily living Fukuyama's dream of the 1990s in which Coca-Cola, indeed, became more 'real' than 'real existing' socialism, everything suddenly became 'absolute fake' – not just 'real existing socialism', but also 'real existing capitalism'.

But what if it was precisely Chernobyl that brought the Western and Soviet ideologies closer than ever even before the fall of the Wall – namely, the ideology of 'peaceful' nuclear energy (as opposed to 'military use') embodied in the Walt Disney mass-market paperback (1956) and TV film (1957) called *Our Friend the Atom*, and still visible in the famous letters on a building in Pripyat saying in Russian 'Let the atom be a worker, not a soldier'? These were originally the words of Soviet nuclear physicist Igor Kurchatov, known as the father of the Soviet atomic bomb, who later advocated peaceful development of nuclear technology, the so-called 'peaceful atom' (*mirnyi atom*). Today we know that both the United States and the Soviet Union constructed the fake dichotomy between military and peaceful use of nuclear technology, and while in public they were comforting their populations through various propaganda, the superpowers – as we will soon see in the next chapter – were at the same time exploring and testing the political use of nuclear energy.

So to come back to Kosolapov's famous *Lenin Coca-Cola* and its underlying message that 'real existing socialism' was turning into 'real existing capitalism': what if precisely this has to be applied to the Chernobyl Power Plant itself, whose official name was, indeed, *Vladimir Ilyich Lenin* Nuclear Power Plant? And how did we come from Lenin to Chernobyl, from an emancipatory idea (as Lenin's famous slogan said, 'Communism is Soviet power + electrification of the entire country') to the total fiasco of Soviet bureaucracy that was supposed to provide all Russia with cheap electricity but instead led to the spreading of dangerous radioactivity? And, again, is there really a big difference between the former East and the West when it comes to nuclear technology?

What if the fundamentally incompetent bureaucracy and corrupted political *nomenklatura* of the radiant communist future was nothing but a mirror of the Western radiant counterpart that would manifest itself in nuclear testings in the Marshall Islands and the nuclear disaster of Fukushima, or with Donald Trump's administration wanting to reclassify leaking nuclear waste as less dangerous so that the government could save billions of dollars and decades of work?[51] What if the disaster of Chernobyl is nothing compared to the possible future unleashed by a crazy Western leader – the same one who didn't understand the wind – who even suggested 'nuking hurricanes' (*really!*) to stop them hitting the United States?[52] Then, as if this wasn't dystopian enough, at the peak of the COVID-19 pandemic in May 2020, the Trump administration started to consider a return to nuclear testing after a 28-year hiatus.[53]

This is the true meaning of 'Enjoy Chernobyl, die later' – namely, the fact that instead of thinking about future generations that will have to deal with the radiant future and nuclear waste, it is important to 'enjoy now', even if it's in the perverse universe of Donald Trump of 'nuking hurricanes' – because later we are going to die anyhow. The 'real thing' of *Lenin Coca-Cola*, which would find its new expression in the current touristic commodification of Chernobyl but also of the coming (literal) 'end of history' (a global nuclear catastrophe would really end all ideologies and thus also *history* as such), was nothing else but another version of Günther Anders's proclamation 'Chernobyl is everywhere'.

The fact that today we can visit Chernobyl, walk around the 'Exclusion Zone' with a dosimeter measuring and warning us about the higher levels of radioactivity, that we can even have a vegetarian meal in the 'socialist' cantina of the *Vladimir Ilyich Lenin* Nuclear Power Plant and, that we can, as of October 2019, also visit (at least for a few minutes because of the highly dangerous radiation levels) the notorious control room of Reactor 4[54] doesn't make the Apocalypse more 'real'. Even if the Apocalypse is commodified and *memento consumo* has become our new *memento mori*, as probably everyone among the 100,000 tourists who visited the 'Exclusion Zone' in 2019 knows, there is still something left, something that is beyond commodification, something that cannot be commodified – 'the real thing'. And even if we can see the deserted buildings and streets, namely the effects of the nuclear disaster, this 'real' remains invisible and 'unreal'.

When we are faced with the radiant present of the 'Exclusion Zone', it is as if the message 'It's the Real Thing. Lenin' becomes 'Chernobyl. It's the Unreal

Thing'. It could be undersigned by Günther Anders, who else? It is not only 'unreal' because the experience of the post-Apocalypse is commodified by being 'staged' and 'mediated'. It is also 'unreal' because the very experience of visiting the 'Exclusion Zone' is *supral-iminal* – it exceeds the ordinary human experience and our neuronal capacity. This is, among other things, because radioactivity as a threat is 'invisible'. And nowhere was it more (un)real, in a horrific and tragic way, then in Svetlana Alexievich's *Voices from Chernobyl* and the numerous descriptions of encounters with the 'invisible' threat that suddenly appeared among people who were losing their loved ones. Like the following:

> There's a fragment of some conversation, I'm remembering it. Someone is saying: 'You have to understand: this is not your husband anymore, not a beloved person, but a radioactive object with a strong density of poisoning. You're not suicidal. Get ahold of yourself.' And I'm like someone who's lost her mind: 'But I love him! I love him!' He's sleeping, I'm whispering: 'I love you!' Walking in the hospital courtyard, 'I love you.' Carrying his sanitary tray, 'I love you.'[55]

Radioactivity is *supraliminal* whether you encounter it in your loved one (who is, just like in the old science fiction film *Invasion of the Bodysnatchers*, not the same person anymore) or you are faced with a place that is radioactive like today's Chernobyl open to post-apocalyptic tourism. Even when I was standing in front of the notorious 'Sarcophagus', the gigantic 36,000-ton steel containment arch that is covering Reactor 4 and is one of the largest moveable land-based structures in the world, it was still somewhat 'unreal'. And the longer I was standing there, it wasn't becoming any more real; on the contrary, it was becoming a sinister materialization of 'real existing' science fiction. Even if I could record unthreatening levels of radioactivity outside it with my dosimeter, and I knew that there are around 200 tonnes of highly radioactive material inside the 'sarcophagus', it looked like a pyramid, a truly post-apocalyptic site that was going beyond the limits of comprehension. Even if it was real and in front of me, it was too big to fully understand it. It was supraliminal. No wonder one soldier in *Voices from Chernobyl* called it 'a twentieth-century pyramid'.[56]

3

The Collision: Marshall Islands Are Everywhere

Here among the blocks you at last find an image of yourself free of the hazards of time and space. This island is an ontological Garden of Eden, why seek to expel yourself into a world of quantal flux?'

J. G. Ballard, *The Terminal Beach*, 1964

'The ontological Garden of Eden'

Perhaps there is no better way to understand what it means to live 'after the Apocalypse' than to imagine a place in the midst of the Pacific Ocean, a chain of volcanic islands halfway between Hawaii and Australia. Located north of the equator, this place spreads over an area roughly the size of Indonesia or Mexico. For thousands of years the indigenous communities of these 1,200 islands, scattered across 750,000 square miles of ocean, have managed to survive and thrive on the waters, with skilled navigation and sophisticated knowledge about waves and winds, developing a common culture on this vast territory and constructing a large ocean state called the Marshall Islands.

Together with other islands in the Pacific Ocean, like
the globally more famous 'tourist heaven' Maldives, or
lesser known Kiribati and Tuvalu, the Marshall Islands
were among the first victims of climate crisis. While in
other parts of the world, sea-level rise was perhaps still
seen as a sort of distant future, the sea around these
islands has already risen two or three times faster than
the global average since 1990.[1] In recent years, most
of these islands have already been fortifying shorelines
and building coastal protections, strengthening water
and food security. But none of that seems sufficient
in face of the eschatological threat they are facing in
the twenty-first century. There are as many as 30,000
islands between the United States and Japan that are
struggling with severe climate disruption, but what
makes the future of the Marshall Islands even more
frightening unveils itself in the image that you can see
on the cover of this book.

If you haven't come across this image before, and
know nothing about it, it could even appear as an
abstract painting with perfect shapes and calming
colours. Close the book and observe it again: what if
this beautiful aerial image of something that appears
as structured harmony is nothing more nor less than a
perfect illustration of the world 'after the Apocalypse'?
And what if precisely this image – or rather, the reality
captured in it, which is at the same time hidden – represents an ominous 'revelation' of the ontological and
metaphysical abyss we are facing today? If there ever
was a more dreadful embodiment of the destruction
and self-destruction of late *Homo sapiens*, it is this
image. On the one side, you can see a crater caused by
nuclear testing; on the other, there is a concrete dome
with buried nuclear waste that the Marshallese simply
call – 'the Tomb'.

Never have the past and the future, the bomb and
the tomb, been juxtaposed in such a frightening way:

that what has been, what created the crater, is literally waiting to happen again – it actually never went away, it was just buried in a protective 'Tomb' whose architects didn't take into account the rising sea levels in the same way the architects of Venice's MOSE projected a structure for a world that no longer exists. And, just like Freud's 'return of the repressed', that which is buried is always waiting to return in a much more sinister way. What happens when the Tomb of the bomb, all that nuclear waste buried below the greyish concrete structure, leaks into the oceans due to rapidly rising sea levels? Moreover, what if the 'outside' of the Tomb is no longer really an 'outside', because the inside (radioactivity) is already outside (in the ocean), and the outside (the ocean) is already inside (penetrating the structure with buried radioactivity)? In short, what the image on the cover of this book embodies is the collision of the nuclear age and climate crisis, it is the image of 'After the Apocalypse'.

It all started in June 1946 when, less than a year after Hiroshima and Nagasaki, the United States started testing nuclear weapons in and above the Marshall Islands – a place that, given how radioactive it is, could be described as the 'ground zero' of the nuclear age. As Greg Dvorak noted, a professor of history and culture in Tokyo who spent his childhood in Kwajalein Atoll (part of the Marshall Islands), it is 'uncanny' that the word 'Marshall' – the name of a British sea captain John Marshall, after whom the islands were named on European maps in the nineteenth century – should be homophonic with the term 'martial'. Indeed, as Dvorak warns, 'throughout the last century these islands were used as stepping-stones to accomplish the military agendas of the world superpowers'.[2]

At the time of the nuclear testings, the famous American comedian Bob Hope made a grim joke: 'As soon as the war ended, we found the one spot on Earth

Figure 6: Nuclear testing at Bikini Atoll, 'Castle Bravo', 1954

that had been untouched by war and blew it to hell.'[3] That wasn't quite true, since the Pacific islands were already a battleground for the United States and Japan during the Second World War. But with 67 nuclear tests conducted between 1946 and 1958 at the Bikini and Enewatak atolls, it's undoubtedly the most nuked place in this part of the universe. In fact, if the combined explosive power of all the tests in the archipelago of the Marshall Islands was parcelled evenly over that 12-year period, it would equal 1.6 Hiroshima-size explosions per day.[4] This is the true dimension of supraliminality that Günther Anders was talking about, something that is so big that it becomes impossible to think about it.

Just take the detonation of the thermonuclear weapon test called 'Castle Bravo' at the Bikini Atoll in March 1954, which was the most powerful artificial explosion in history at that time. Although only its inventor knows what the name 'Castle Bravo' was referring to, once it exploded, this 'castle' of 15 megatons of TNT vaporized parts of the Marshall Islands, with temperatures hitting as high as 55,000°C. Within just one minute, the gigantic mushroom cloud, consisting of pulverized radioactive coral, reached a height of around 15 kilometres, breaking 30 kilometres two minutes later.[5] Six minutes later, the cloud top rose and peaked at almost 40 kilometres. 'Castle Bravo' was expanding at an enormous speed of more than 100 metres per second (around 360km/h), and eight minutes after the detonation, the mushroom cloud reached its full dimensions with a diameter of 100 kilometres. This single detonation was 1,000 times more powerful than either one of the atomic bombs that were dropped on Hiroshima and Nagasaki.[6]

The nuclear fallout of the exploded 'castle', which some of the islanders mistook for snow just before they suffered skin burns, hair loss and, eventually, cancer, contaminated more than 18,000 square kilometres of the surrounding Pacific Ocean, while traces of radio-active material reached as far as Japan, Australia and India, and even the United States and parts of Europe. Recently, researchers from Columbia University found that the radioactivity of soil on the atolls of the Marshall Islands where the nuclear tests had been conducted greatly exceeds radioactivity levels near Chernobyl and Fukushima. At the spot of the Castle Bravo detonation, those levels are reported to be 1,000 times higher.[7]

The scope and effects of this whole operation, including the effects of other powerful nuclear weapons tests, were revealed only recently. In November 2019, investigative journalists from the *Los Angeles Times*, Carolyn Cole and Susanne Rust, made several trips to document the ongoing devastation of the Marshall Islands' 'Runit Dome', which holds more than 3.1 million cubic feet (87,800 cubic metres) of toxic nuclear waste (including plutonium). To visualize this size, the journalists invite us to imagine 35 Olympic-sized swimming pools full of radioactive soil and debris, including lethal amounts of plutonium.[8] Even if we succeed in picturing this by comparing it to familiar parameters (Olympic-sized swimming pools), even if we have a realistic photograph of the Marshall Islands in front of our eyes (such as the cover image of this book), can we really ever fully grasp this 'ontological Tomb'? Namely, what is taking place here, beneath the structure that is already being submerged into the ocean, is a profound ontological change in the very nature of being, something that is not only affecting humans and nature, but also space and time.

What is unfolding here is 'supraliminal' – it is the collision of climate crisis and the nuclear age. Just as the sinking and leaking 'Tomb' eliminates the difference between the 'inside' and the 'outside', so the Marshall Islands remind us that the effects of climate crisis and the nuclear age are intertwined as never before.

What is simultaneously present here are two eschatological threats that are, once and for all, blurring the difference between 'inside' and 'outside'; on the one hand toxic radioactivity, on the other rising sea levels. According to a report commissioned by the US Department of Defense and published quietly in March 2018, the islands are expected to be entirely submerged by seawater at least once a year from 2035.[9] This report was, in the first place, commissioned not because the American military was concerned about the nuclear waste repository and rising sea levels, but because it was worried that Kwajalein Island – which after the Second World War became the main command centre for the nuclear tests at the Marshall Islands and today serves as a spot for missile tests of all sorts (including the first commercial Falcon rockets launched by Elon Musk's SpaceX)[10] – would face rapid and frequent sea level rises and the salt water will destroy the expensive equipment and infrastructure of this multibillion-dollar US military installation.

The peer-reviewed 138-page study commissioned by the US Department of Defense took four years to complete and cost millions of dollars. Researchers went to one of the atolls of the Marshall Islands and concluded that climate crisis will make the islands literally uninhabitable in 15 years. But after the scientists published the report, there was no distributed press release. This sort of approach would be quite unusual for a 'revelation' of this magnitude if it hadn't been unveiled during a tragic moment in American politics, when officials of the Interior Department, fearful of contradicting Donald Trump's view on climate crisis, would even decide to remove any mention of 'climate change' from another press release on a study about sea-level rise.[11]

Already in early December 2019, this prediction was coming true when Majuro, the capital of the Marshall

Islands, was flooded and its population witnessed the largest recorded outbreak of dengue fever on the islands. While the *Los Angeles Times* was reporting that 'Huge waves and disease turn Marshall Islands into "a war zone"',[12] the then Marshall Islands president Hilda Heine, speaking over a video link from the climate 'warzone' at the meeting of international leaders at the United Nation's Climate conference in Madrid, warned the world: 'As we speak, hundreds of people have evacuated their homes as the large waves caused the ocean to inundate parts of our capital in Majuro last week. As a nation we refuse to flee. But we also refuse to die.'[13]

These are the disastrous effects of the collision of the nuclear age and climate crisis. The citizens of the Marshall Islands had already been forced to relocate from one island to another because of the nuclear testings; in the meantime, one-third of the population left the atolls,[14] and they are now once again facing relocation because of rising sea levels. As a low-lying atoll island nation – little more than one metre above sea level – the Marshall Islands represent the literal 'ground zero' of the collision of eschatological threats that are no longer just lying dormant in a far-off science fiction future, but actually exist in a real dystopian present. 'That dome', as the Marshall Islands climate activist Alson Kelen said in November 2017, 'is the connection between the nuclear age and the climate age.'[15]

The collision of the nuclear age and climate crisis

If we look at the map of the world from the perspective of geology, what we can see today is that the Pacific Ocean, including the Marshall Islands as well as thousands of other islands, is nothing more – nor less – than the result of an earlier major cataclysm, a gigantic and long-lasting geological change that can be traced back 750 million years to when the Panthalassic Ocean was first formed out of the split of the Proterozoic continent Rodinia. In the meantime, during a period that took millions of years, the supercontinent Pangea began to develop, before it too, just like Rodinia, begun to fragment, resulting in the formation of the central Atlantic Ocean (180 million years ago), the Pacific Ocean (167 million years ago) and the Indian Ocean, leading to India separating from Madagascar (140 million years ago). Only 50 million years ago did the Earth start to attain its current form and the arrangement of oceans and continents that we can see on the map of the world today.

To cut a really long story rather short, from the perspective of geology, the Pacific Ocean and its islands came about as a result of a colossal previous catastrophe, or series of catastrophes, including shifting of plates, gigantic earthquakes, volcanic eruptions and major changes in sea levels. But what we are encountering on the Marshall Islands today is something much more sinister. First, because, unlike the dinosaurs who couldn't do anything about the asteroid hitting Earth, we are ourselves responsible for the collision. And second, because we as humans have the neural capacity to think about this eschatological threat that is leading to a major geological change that is already profoundly transforming the Pacific Ocean – and, in fact, the whole planet. However, even if this planetary catastrophe appears 'supraliminal', beyond all the ends we have encountered or imagined before (not just a nuclear disaster but also climate catastrophe at the very same time), couldn't we say that humans already encountered a similar 'sense of an ending' even before the current collision between the climate and nuclear catastrophes embodied in the Tomb at the Marshall Islands? Moreover, even if the eschatological tipping points we are facing today don't seem to resemble anything humanity has witnessed before, haven't many scientists, writers and activists been able to perceive and imagine the enormity of these threats for years?

'It seems doubtful that our crisis', writes Frank Kermode in his influential *Sense of an Ending*, 'our relation to the future and to the past, is one of the important differences between us and our predecessors. Many of them felt as we do.'[16] This is one of the central points that he developed in a series of lectures he gave in autumn 1965, at the time when the Cuban missile crisis and the assassination of President Kennedy were quite recent events and the world seemed as if it might explode at any given moment. Yet, when we have the image and the reality of the ontological Tomb of the Marshall Islands in front of our eyes, do we really feel like our predecessors and did they really feel like us? And what if it is not so much just about the 'sense of an ending', but about the fact that this is not an end as any other end? It is the end of the very imagination of the end, because after this end there will be no one left to imagine.

What still holds true, as in Kermode's times, is that it is through 'crisis' that we make sense of our world and that we, as humans, always think our own present crisis is more worrying than any other moment in human history. According to Kermode, even if we think of our 'end times' as unique, it is not the first time that humanity has lived through an apocalyptic *Zeitgeist*. For instance, there was a 'sense of an ending' during the *fin de siècle* (the end of the nineteenth century), and during the historical periods of different millennialist movements in the Middle Ages or subsequent secularized forms of apocalypticism (it is well known that the German radical theologian of the early Reformation period Thomas Müntzer influenced such figures as Karl Marx and Ernst Bloch), not to mention the extermination of indigenous people for whom it was

literally the end of the world when they were slaugh-
tered by the colonialists in the 'discovered' Americas.
As Déborah Danowski and Eduardo Viveiros de Castro
remind us in their thoughtful book *The Ends of The
World*, which makes a much-needed anthropological
and philosophical move beyond the usual Western-
centric view, 'indigenous people have something to
teach us when it comes to apocalypses, losses of
world, demographic catastrophes, and ends of History'
because:

> for native people of the Americas, *the end of the world
> already happened* – five centuries ago. To be exact, it
> began on October 12, 1492. (As someone once said
> on Twitter, 'the first Indian to find Columbus made a
> horrible discovery' ...) The indigenous population of
> the continent, larger than that of Europe at that time,
> may have lost – by means of the combined action
> of viruses (smallpox in particular being spectacularly
> lethal), iron, gunpowder, and paper (treaties, papal
> bulls, royal *encomienda* concessions, and of course
> the Bible) – something of the order of 95 percent of its
> bulk throughout the first one and a half centuries of the
> Conquest. That would correspond, according to some
> demographers, to a fifth of the planet's population.[17]

In other words, whenever we speak about the
Apocalypse, we should never forget that the end(s) of
the world already happened. Nevertheless, having the
image of the Marshallese 'ontological Tomb' in front of
us, what if today, as climate crisis and the nuclear age
collide, we are no longer confronted merely with the
'ends of the world', but with an end that will end all
other possible 'ends of the world'? This doesn't mean
that another end of the world is no longer possible:
the world doesn't have to end because of nuclear war
or complete climate breakdown. However, whenever
that end occurs, it will still be the end of 'epochality'

as such. Collision is the absolute *epoché* because after this age there will be no other 'epoch' coming, in the sense of a period of time that was, as long as there was human history, always leading towards a new 'epoch' (*Zeitalter*). After the 'End-Time' there will be no other major epoch of world history simply because there will be no more historicality; it will be the end of human time. If an 'epoch' as an instant in time chosen to fit the modern chronology (*chronos*) and periodization of time usually serves as a reference point from which time is measured (the past and the future), how would we – or more precisely, who would (if there are no humans anymore) – measure time after a total event? An event in the true sense of the word 'total', an event that encompasses the 'whole' not only of humanity, its languages and history, but also other species and the planet, in a way – time itself.

So to come back to Kermode's point that our epoch is perhaps just another epoch after which there will come another epoch with similar eschatological threats: even if what Kermode calls 'authentic crisis-feelings' have been felt by millions of people in the past, and they are surely felt by the billions of people clinging for survival today, what if this epoch isn't replaced by another epoch in history, but perhaps only with a new epoch in the geological sense of the word (something that comes after the Anthropocene itself)? It is not so much a question of a 'sense of an ending' anymore, or noticing the eschatological threat and having 'authentic crisis-feelings'; it is about the very notion of 'epochality' that might be ending due to the collision of the nuclear age and climate breakdown. It is language itself and the ability to imagine a different end that will vanish in the ontological abyss, not just the biosphere as we know it, but the semiosphere as well.

Today, at a time when multiple eschatological threats are in collision, there seems to be an important difference between us and our predecessors. The 'sense of an ending' today is not so much about imagining the end anymore, but about the impossibility of being able to imagine coming even close to the 'supraliminal' nature of the possible near future, or – as in the case of the Marshall Islands – to the future that already happened. This is embodied in the 'Tomb' on the cover image of this book, something that seems almost hyperreal (like a documentary image of the end of the world), but its effects and consequences surpass our cognitive ability to fully grasp it, so it becomes 'unreal'. What is at stake in the times 'after the Apocalypse' is much more than a singular death or even extinction of *Homo sapiens*, as Kermode seems to imply in *The Sense of an Ending*. It is not just an 'existential' anxiety each person feels regarding a possible end; it is an end that will end all senses of an ending, because there will simply be no one to sense anymore.

What makes the Marshall Islands a truly post-apocalyptic case – different from anything our predecessors lived through – is the collision of the nuclear age and climate crisis that will not only affect one place, but that will have been (like Günther Anders's flood, a *futur antérieur*) in all places after the eschatological tipping points have been reached. And it is not just space that will have been affected, but time itself. It will have been in all places at the same time. It will have been a planetary event. The difference today between us and our predecessors, who were undoubtedly having a 'sense of an ending' for millennia and even more, is that we are not just sitting at the top of a super-volcano that is ready to erupt, or that one culture/civilization is about to be annihilated by another. The 'sense of an ending' that we are facing today consists, besides eschatological threats that are completely out of our control (for instance, an asteroid hitting the Earth), in the fact that we are encountering an inevitable and final catastrophe that is perhaps still at least to a certain degree controllable, but that might easily reach its tipping point at any given moment and catapult us into the company of the dinosaurs.

From the perspective of the evolution of the planet and its previous geological changes and mass extinctions (the series of catastrophes that lead to new life and the new life that now leads to a new planetary catastrophe), it is difficult not to agree, once again, with Déborah Danowski and Eduardo Viveiros de Castro, who present us with a much-needed self-reflection on the very meaning of 'being human':

> The idea that our species is a newcomer on the planet, that history as we know it (agriculture, cities, writing) is even more recent, and that the energy-intensive, fossil-fuel based industrial way of life began only a seconds ago in terms of *Homo sapiens'* evolutionary clock all seems to point to the conclusion that humankind itself is a catastrophe: a sudden, devastating event in the planet's biological and geophysical history, one that will disappear much faster than the changes it will have occasioned in the Earth's thermodynamic regime and biological balance.[18]

Today, when we are faced with 'supraliminal' data telling us that, over the past 25 years, the oceans have absorbed heat equivalent to the energy of 3.6 billion Hiroshima-size atom bombs exploding,[19] which then results in more powerful tropical storms and greater suffering, it is difficult not to see humankind itself – as magnificent as it might be from the view-point of evolution – as the catastrophe. Moreover, when we have in mind that the scale of such a planetary event is exacerbated or, in fact, produced by global capitalism that is still relying on the extraction of fossil fuels (itself a result of a previous planetary catastrophe), it is hard not to be tempted to call it – to use Hannah Arendt's famous phrase – 'the banality of the Apocalypse'. It is not 'banal' merely because evil on a planetary scale is being perpetrated by men – 'the Eichmanns of the Apocalypse' – who are part of a global capitalist machinery without conscience, it is 'banal' also because we are all being transformed into 'Eichmann's sons' without even knowing it. This is what Günther Anders asked in a letter addressed to Klaus Eichmann, the son of the notorious Nazi perpetrator of the Holocaust:

> Do you notice something, Klaus Eichmann? Do you notice that the so-called Eichmann problem is not yesterday's problem? That it does not belong to the past? That there is no reason at all for us ... to feel superior to yesterday? That all of us, exactly like you, are confronted by what is too huge for us? ... That all of us are likewise Eichmann's sons? At least sons of the Eichmannian world (*Eichmanwelt*)?[20]

In other words, we are all 'relatives' (*Verwandter*) of Eichmann, children of the one and same epoch, the epoch or 'End-Time' that will become a devastating event in the planet's biological and geophysical history precisely thanks to our conscience – or the absence of it.

When the United States dropped the atomic bomb on Hiroshima, only a year before nuclear testings began in and above the Marshall Islands, according to Günther Anders, what started in the midst of this horrific destruction was not only a new moral epoch in which we would all become 'Eichmann's sons', it was the beginning of a new ontological epoch as well. Anders proclaimed that 'Hiroshima is everywhere', describing it as the dawn of a new time:

> *Hiroshima as World Condition:* On August 6, 1945, the Day of Hiroshima, a New Age began: the age in

which at any given moment we have the power to transform any given place on our planet, and even our planet itself, into a Hiroshima. On that day we became, at least '*modo negativo*', omnipotent; but since, on the other hand, we can be wiped out at any given moment, we also became totally impotent. However long this age may last, even if it should last forever, it is 'The Last Age': for there is no possibility that its '*differentia specifica*', the possibility of our self-extinction, can ever end – but by the end itself.[21]

As we have seen in the previous chapter, Anders warned, when the Chernobyl disaster happened, that 'globocide', namely the destruction of the terraqueous globe, was inevitable because we are unable to 'unlearn' what we know – namely, how to destroy ourselves and the planet (we can't 'unlearn' knowledge about nuclear energy, which itself contains the possibility of a nuclear disaster and self-destruction). 'Hiroshima is everywhere' became 'Chernobyl is everywhere'. Regardless of where it occurs, whether in Chernobyl or Hiroshima, Harrisburg or Fukushima, thanks to just one nuclear disaster, as Anders warned in his 'Ten theses on Chernobyl', 'all the other places of our dear Earth could be transformed simultaneously into an immense Hiroshima, or even into something worse'.[22] Today, when the nuclear age and climate crisis collide, when radioactivity left by nuclear testings and rapidly rising sea levels might be transforming the whole world into an immense Marshall Islands, we should perhaps say: 'Marshall Islands are everywhere'.

It is not just that every place on the planet could be annihilated exactly like Hiroshima or Chernobyl; the current situation as embodied in the Marshall Islands is pointing towards an even more sinister future – or rather present, when it comes to the real existing place in the Pacific Ocean – because not only 'locations in space, but also points in time, will be affected, if they have not already been affected'.[23] And yet, it is as this whole 'revelation' (Apocalypse in its original meaning) remains somewhat 'unreal'. It is not 'unreal' just because the United States government didn't reveal the true effects of its powerful nuclear tests or has censored the 'revelation' about rising sea levels, it is 'unreal' because the very image of the ontological 'Tomb', even if we can describe it or imagine what is below, even if we can close this book once again and take another glance at the cover image, simply remains beyond our comprehension. If the 'sarcophagus' of Chernobyl was called the pyramid of the twentieth century, then the Marshall Islands – and more specifically, the 'Runit Dome' on the Enewetak Atoll – should be called the pyramids of the twenty-first century.

The twenty-first-century pyramids

It is here where Chernobyl and the Marshall Islands, the previous chapter and this chapter, finally meet, namely in the question of what will be left 'after the Apocalypse', after the nuclear disaster or after the collision, what will have happened to all the nuclear waste or radioactivity, whether it was produced by nuclear testings or by nuclear power plant disasters, once the world has reached the climate tipping point, not to mention the possibility of a nuclear war. In the previous chapter, we explored how Chernobyl became a post-apocalyptic tourist 'heaven' with a 'sarcophagus' that is designed to contain radiation for only another 100 years. What we encounter in the Pacific 'paradise' is even more sinister: it is a place being swallowed by rising sea levels with toxic nuclear waste already leaking and being submerged into the Pacific Ocean.

What brings both together is not only the already existing contamination, it is also the future contamination. This is why the soldier from *Voices from Chernobyl* was right to compare the 'sarcophagus' to the pyramids. Because what else are places such as Chernobyl and the Marshall Islands but 'pyramids' of a sort, perhaps the only 'monuments' of human civilization (its radioactivity) that will still exist in 10,000 or even 24,000 years? If even 4,500 years after the famous Giza Pyramids were built we are still not able to fully comprehend them, what guarantee is there that some future archaeologist will be able to understand our contemporary nuclear 'pyramids'? And unlike today, when everyone is occupied by the short-term perspective and destroying the world as quickly as possible, it is precisely these sorts of questions – how to communicate the 'revelation' (about the dangers of buried or leaking radioactivity) to future generations – that were being raised by the US Department of Energy and the Bechtel Group, the conglomerate in charge of maintaining and securing several nuclear facilities in the United States. Back in 1981, they invited a team of linguists, semioticians, anthropologists and nuclear physicists to explore how to reduce the likelihood of future interference in radioactive waste repositories. The prime objective of this grand initiative of applied 'nuclear semiotics', which had to take into account also the possibility that over such a long period spoken and written languages might go extinct, was to come up with concrete proposals of how to transmit knowledge about the repositories to future generations. To put it simply, how do we prevent some future archaeologists from thinking that they have found the Giza pyramids of our time?

The so-called Human Interference Task Force concluded that significant reductions in the likelihood of human interference could be achieved, for perhaps thousands of years into the future, if appropriate steps are taken to communicate the existence of the repository.

Consequently, the Task Force directed most of its study for two years towards the field of long-term communication. Around the same time, in order to determine how to convey such a message to a distant future, the German *Zeitschrift für Semiotik* carried out a survey in 1982 asking the following question: 'How would it be possible to inform our descendants for the next 10,000 years about the storage locations and dangers of radioactive waste?'[24] The responses, even though the period of 10,000 years seems a rather optimistic projection of how long nuclear waste would stay radioactive, were highly original and thought-provoking, even from today's perspective. And the more we head out into the one-way street of planetary catastrophe, the more interesting – and important – they are becoming. Because they open up the terrain of the long-term perspective that is so absent today, and, at the same time, a sense of urgency – but also come up with solutions that would until recently have been dismissed as science fiction – when it comes to thinking about the transmission of knowledge and intergenerational solidarity.

For instance, the American semiotician and linguist Thomas Sebeok, one of the founders of 'zoosemiotics' and 'biosemiotics',[25] who was a member of the Human Interference Task Force in the early 1980s, proposed the creation of what he called an 'Atomic Priesthood', a panel composed of scientists (physicists, anthropologists, semioticians) that would, like the major religious institutions (for example, the Catholic Church), have the obligation to preserve and chronicle the 'warning' over the next 2,000 years (in this case, not the biblical 'revelation', but the message about the dangers and locations of the radioactive waste). How would they do it? In his detailed report for the US Office of Nuclear Waste Management, titled 'Communication measures to bridge ten millennia', Sebeok proposes a 'folkloric relay system', basically suggesting that the 'Atomic

Priesthood', after dividing the 10,000-year frame into manageable segments of shorter periods, should deal with creating annually renewed rituals and legends retold year-on-year.[26]

The Polish science fiction author Stanisław Lem, famous for his novel *Solaris* (1961), proposed the creation of artificial satellites that would transmit the warning from their orbit to Earth for millennia and, just in case, would encode information about the nuclear waste into the DNA of flowers to be planted near the repositories. The German physicist and author Philipp Sonntag went a step further and suggested constructing an artificial moon that would last for 10,000 years engraved with the warning message.[27] And certainly one of the most thought-provoking proposals, based on evidence of the long history of coexistence between cats and humans, a French author together with an Italian semiotician proposed breeding 'radiation cats' that would change colour when they went near radioactive sites.[28]

In 1984, after two years of interdisciplinary delib-eration across the world, the Human Interference Task Force published a substantial technical report for the US Department of Energy containing their final proposal.[29] None of the above proposals entered the final report, and instead of zoosemiotics or engineering a new religion to protect nuclear waste repositories, the Task Force proposed an architectural – or rather 'place-making' – solution, namely, the creation of a large monument at the site formed out of several gigantic stone monoliths inscribed with the information in all human languages. It is an interesting solution, but the same question remains: how to communicate (the 'revelation') across millennia so that it could be read and decoded, and what if – in that distant future – there is no one to communicate with?

Almost a decade after the report of the Human Interference Task Force, these questions about how to communicate with the wholly uncertain future were still not solved, and the US Department of Energy convened another group in 1993 to help redesign the nuclear warning messages for the Waste Isolation Pilot Plant (WIPP) in New Mexico, which would become the first operational deep geological repository in the USA in 1999. In the so-called Sandia Report, one of the groups of scientists also adopted an architectural approach and proposed a sort of monument consisting of 'menacing earthworks' and 'spike fields' – giant spikes sticking out in all directions that would serve as warning signs for future generations.[30] It was a truly 'place-making' proposal; much more than just an architectural design, it implied creating an experience that would guide future explorers through its successive layers until they had understood the warning and the threat buried deep inside the ground.[31]

Similar to the worries in the United States, one of Europe's most committed nuclear nation-states, with 58 reactors producing 75 per cent of the country's power – namely, France – also encountered the same problem with its toxic radioactive waste, which, according to the *Financial Times*, could annually fill 120 double-decker buses (about 13,000 cubic metres worth, or 2 kilograms a year for every French person).[32] While in the 1970s and 1980s nuclear agencies in France were, in fact, already exploring the possibilities of rocketing nuclear waste into space or putting it deep in the ocean, since the 1990s France seems to have opted for the solution of burying the radioactive waste in deep underground repositories, just like many other countries in the world. But if you bury it under the ground, you are back to the question of how to warn future generations of the eschatological threat.

To find an answer to this question (or perhaps to rebrand the 'security' of the repositories), the French nuclear waste agency Andra launched a competition in

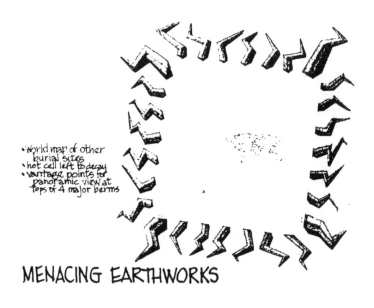

• world map of other
  burial sites
• hot cell left to decay
• vantage points for
  panoramic view at
  tops of 4 major berms

MENACING EARTHWORKS

Figure 7: Nuclear waste warnings; concept art by Michael Brill, Sandia National Laboratories

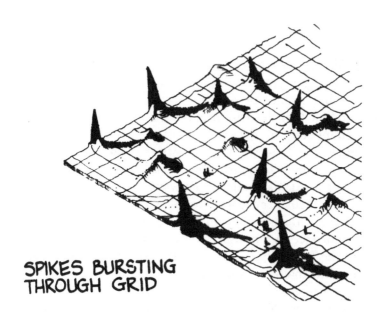

SPIKES BURSTING
THROUGH GRID

2015 for artists to propose how to keep the memory about the threat alive. An Italian composer came up with the idea of children's songs telling the story of where the French waste is buried, reminding us of the importance of story-telling and the oral tradition, while a French artist proposed a biosemiotic solution reminiscent of the 'radiant cats', namely a plan to cover the Bure site with plants that had been genetically modified to turn blue. In the end, the first prize went to Alexis Pandellé's *Prométhée oublié* ('Forgotten Prometheus'), an enormous scar on the ground. One of the problems that all these projects, once realized, might face in the future is, again, the commodification of the Apocalypse – what if even the warning messages become major artistic and architectural wonders not so much of a world to come, but of our own collapsing world that will find a source of profit even in its own self-destruction?

Why are these speculative attempts to construct a message for the future still relevant today? Not just because we have even more nuclear waste than ever before and the 'Doomsday Clock' of the Bulletin of the Atomic Scientists has, for the first time, been set at 100 seconds to midnight (the future is, indeed being counted in seconds, and not years anymore). It is, rather, because the very terrain of questions opened up in the field of 'nuclear semiotics' brings us back to the exploration of intergenerational change and continuity, the responsibility for the distant future that is becoming the single most important task of our generation.

Yet, with the collision of the nuclear age and climate crisis, the ruins from the future are not the same as the ruins from the past: the ruins of Pompeii or Rome are perhaps still 'sublime' because they bear witness to human 'progress' and how we outlived even those 'ends of the world', although, instead of 'progress' it would be better – like in Walter Benjamin's vision of the Angelus Novus – to call it the human ability to create new ruins again and again. However, what if our current predicament is much more sinister than Benjamin's deconstruction of 'progress'? What if, after the Apocalypse, after the collision of the nuclear age and climate catastrophe, there is no 'Angel of History', simply because there will be no history anymore? And there will be no history, because there would, literally, be no survivor. Not just no one to recall. But nothing to recall. It would, indeed, be the last epoch and the end of 'epochality' as such, because our reality would – as Günther Anders called it – become an *Apocalypse without kingdom*, a sort of 'naked Apocalypse'. There is nothing to come after the last epoch, because there will be no other epoch, we can only continue living in the 'End-Time' (*Endzeit*) and perhaps create a different end of the world. Unlike the optimistic thesis of 'kingdom without Apocalypse', what the thesis of the 'naked Apocalypse without kingdom' opens up is an ontological abyss.

Or, as Anders puts it in an important description of this new sort of eschatology:

'No matter how lively the concept 'apocalypse' (transformed into the concept 'revolution') had become for them, the concept of the 'kingdom' was no less lively. The schemas of Judeo-Christian eschatology 'demise and justice' or 'end and kingdom' shone very clearly through the Communist doctrine, with the revolution playing the role of the apocalypse, and the classless society playing the role of 'the kingdom of god'. Furthermore, the idea of the revolution, which represented the apocalypse, didn't mean an event that just fell from the sky, but rather an action that would have been downright senseless if it didn't usher in the goal of the 'kingdom'. So there can be no talk of an affinity with the concepts we are required to think through today: the 'naked apocalypse without kingdom'. Conversely, in light of the possibility of a total catastrophe we face today, Marx and Paul seem to become contemporaries. Those differences which had previously marked out the fronts – even the fundamental distinction – between theism and atheism seem to be condemned to collapse as well.[33]

To live 'after the Apocalypse' carries with it precisely this utter inability to communicate the 'revelation' because there won't be any new 'kingdom' after the Apocalypse, and even the differences between theism and atheism will collapse. It is even possible that the very meaning of *apokalyptein* will be lost, because there will simply be no one left to whom the secret – which we buried deep inside the ground or which is leaking into the oceans – could be 'uncovered'. Not because we didn't want to transmit this precious knowledge – there were indeed original attempts to do it, such as the Human Interference Task Force – but because we have to construct messages that need to outlive tens of thousands of years. At the same time, as supraliminal as this temporality appears, it is precisely such a long-term perspective that can be helpful in preventing a fully radiant future unleashed by the pyramids of the twenty-first century.

Time beyond progress

From an exploration of the future of places – the Mediterranean, Chernobyl, the Marshall Islands – it is here where we finally switch from space and arrive at the notion of 'time' that is always connected to the Apocalypse. In fact, this final stop of our post-apocalyptic journey, which started in the Mediterranean and brought us into the middle of the Pacific Ocean, confronts us with a frightening yet fascinating question:

are language, semiotics or architecture capable of trans-
mitting such a message – the 'revelation' about our
nuclear and climate ruins – into the distant future?
Into a future in which it is possible that no humans or
extraterrestrials will be able to decipher this encrypted
message from the past, a future in which it is also
possible that there are no humans and a future in which
an eschatological event out of human control might
unleash all the 'buried' radioactivity and make the
planet completely uninhabitable for thousands of years.

There are only uncertainties about the pyramids
of the twenty-first century – what if the whole Earth
becomes a nuclear ruin? Wouldn't the theory of 'ruin
value' thus, finally, become obsolete? If there is no one
to see the 'menacing earthworks' and 'spike fields', the
'radiant cats' and 'atomic flowers', what's the point of
these ruins? In order to understand such a future, we
finally have to shift from the spatial perspective to the
temporal one. Besides thinking of the future of places,
namely the spatial futurability, we also have to think
of time itself, that is of the relation between space and
time, between the Apocalypse and temporality. What
brings Noah's Ark and the pyramids of the twenty-first
century together, what connects both repositories – the
one with all the saved species and the one with toxic
nuclear waste – is precisely temporality. Even though
it is undoubtedly a demanding and mind-boggling
architectural and place-making endeavour to construct
for an uncertain future, we are arriving not so much at
the question whether these constructions can withhold
the test of time, but whether language – and culture –
can survive thousands of years. To reinvent the spatial
perspective, but also the temporal perspective, means
understanding the Marshall Islands as a place that is not
only everywhere, but in every time, or rather a catastrophe that is – all the time.

This seems to be the point that the science fiction writer

J. G. Ballard developed in his short post-apocalyptic and melancholic story 'The Terminal Beach', written in 1964. It is a story about solitude and mourning set in the ruins of the nuclear age. A former military pilot named Traven, after losing his wife and son, finds refuge on Enewetak, the very same atoll in the Marshall Islands where in 1979 the Runit Dome would be constructed and left to decay, now being threatened by rapid sea-level rise. Enewetak is an embodiment of what Ballard calls the 'Pre-Third' age, the years before the inevitable Third World War, characterized 'above all by its moral and psychological inversions, by its sense of the whole of history, and in particular of the immediate future ... suspended from the quivering volcano's lip of World War III'.[34] Sometimes in the evenings, Traven would see the spectres of his wife and son among dunes of the island, and he would finally understand their death as part of a bigger destruction: 'Even the death of his wife and six-year-old son in a motor accident seemed only part of this immense synthesis of the historical and psychic zero, the frantic highways where each morning they met their deaths the advance causeways to the global Armageddon.'

The island – Enewetak Atoll – that would later become the place of the nuclear 'Tomb' that is now disappearing into the Pacific Ocean is described as a 'zone of non-time' and as 'doorways into another continuum'. Time doesn't appear to be linear here. The nuclear universe, as Ballard understood very well, rather looks like a version of Salvador Dali's *The Persistence of Memory* (1931), with the famous melting clocks and a landscape that remains consistent. Later in the story, in a section titled 'The Catechism of Goodbye', time becomes quantal: 'For hours it would be noon, the shadows contained within the blocks, the heat reflected off the concrete floor.' Traven then bids his goodbye to Enewetak, Los Alamos, Hiroshima, Alamogordo, and, each time, in 'a flicker of light' each of the blocks, 'like a counter on an abacus ... is plucked away', creating in his mind 'a small interval of neutral space'. This 'megathlon farewell' brings Ballard's post-apocalyptic hero close to another hero we encountered already in the first chapter of this book in the seemingly peaceful Mediterranean, namely Günther Anders's Noah.

While Noah is mourning 'tomorrow's dead today', Traven is coming to terms with the reality of World War III. His act, as delusional as it might seem, is a form of mourning for the future. In fact, Ballard describes the post-apocalyptic lagoon as 'an Auschwitz of the soul whose mausoleums contained the mass graves of the still undead'. In other words, the Marshall Islands is a place of the future, a glimpse of what will happen not only after the nuclear Armageddon, but after – as we should add today – the collision between the nuclear age and climate crisis. After this planetary event, not only will the clocks have melted, but also the landscape won't remain consistent, as we can already see in the Marshall Islands today. It is not so much *The Persistence of Memory* anymore; it is becoming *The Disintegration of the Persistence of Memory* (1954), Dali's later reworking of his previous painting, where space itself seems to be disintegrating.

The name Ballard gives to this place where mind, space and time fuse into one is the 'ontological Garden of Eden', which is his term for a perverted 'paradise'. Written even before the full scope of nuclear testings would become known and more than a decade before the 'ontological Tomb' would be erected in Enewetak, which is now disappearing undersea, Ballard's 'ontological Garden of Eden' can be read as another version of Anders's 'naked Apocalypse'. The 'zone of non-time' where Traven finds himself is perhaps one of the best literary versions of the 'Apocalypse without kingdom', a place where reality itself becomes like a surreal Dali painting. The Marshall Islands are the harbingers of this future, a place where the Apocalypse already happened. It was first, and continuously over the years, 'unveiled' in the nuclear mushrooms above the islands. Then it was lived through by the local population being evacuated, suffering or dying of cancer. Now it is being 'unveiled' in the rising sea levels that will, once the radioactivity is submerged into the sea, change the very nature of being, thus ontology itself.

And it is in this dystopian 'ontological Garden of Eden', a place in which space and time are dissolved, that we arrive to an eschatology that goes beyond the reductionist linear notion of time embodied in the capitalist understanding of 'progress'. It is here, at a place where, over a 12-year period, 1.6 Hiroshima-size explosions per day happened, and which is now vanishing into the depths of the Pacific Ocean, where the notion of 'progress' disintegrates into pieces. Or, to be more precise, what becomes evident (or 'unveiled') here is that progress and catastrophe are, always, two sides of the same coin. And very often, one person's progress is another person's catastrophe. On the one hand, the Marshall Islands are, like so many other islands in the world, being swallowed by rising seas precisely because of the greenhouse gas emissions produced by leading industrial countries of the twenty-first century, such as the United States (and many other 'developed' countries). At the same time, the existing and future contamination of this Pacific 'Garden of Eden' is a direct result of the industrial-military complex of the United States that presented the nuclear testings as 'progress'. In fact, since the atomic bomb was developed, 'progress' has consisted in further perfecting it. After it was dropped on Hiroshima and Nagasaki, the 'perfection' continued through nuclear testings. And the more you perfect a tool that is capable of ending life on Earth, the more this eschatological threat becomes real, it becomes permanent – a world condition. In other words, 'progress' could be called our perfection of the tools of mass extinction. Or to paraphrase Benjamin, there is no document of *progress* that is not at the same time a document of *extinction*.

There is an incredible short propaganda movie called *Bikini – The Atom Island* from 1946 that captures precisely this relation between progress and extinction in a frightening way.[35] It was made just before the nuclear testings called *Operation Crossroads* would start, showing an American soldier on the Bikini Attol as he explains to the local population gathered on the sandy beach below the coconut trees why they have to leave the island. The man, who appeared from nowhere with his big ships, aeroplanes and the H-bomb, simply says: 'The United States government now wants to turn this great destructive force [the atomic bomb] into something good for mankind and these experiments here at Bikini are the first step towards this direction.'

As we see the local population packing and carrying their modest and simple belongings to the ships that will evacuate them to another atoll, we can hear the words of the narrator in the movie:

> They [United States] chose tiny remote Bikini because of its excellent anchorage and because of its complete geographic isolation. The very nature of Bikini as a place on the face of our vast and troubled planet will enable the joint army/navy task force to obtain the maximum information in these tests. Out of that horrifying instant, when this quiet peaceful atoll is transformed into a hellish roaring blast of ghastly power, will come lessons that may determine the basic facts of atomic warfare, the future design of ships and aircraft and the development of defense measures should atomic warfare ever be used against the United States. And far more than this, for concealed within the fiery terror that is the atomic bomb are hidden the

broader and nobler aspects of its mystery, the power for good rather than evil, the ability to save not destroy mankind, to build him a whole new world of atomically powered peace, it is to this glorious opportunity that the humble Bikinians are contributing their little all. I wonder would you so readily give up your everything?

In the next scene of this Ballardian 'Pre-Third age' movie, we see each family of the local population marking the coconut trees on an island that will soon turn into a place out of time, a place 'after the Apocalypse'. They believed they would be able to return home within a short time. But they were relocated from island to island, many of them starving and dying of cancer, some of them returning only in 1970 to find a desert in the place that was supposed to be the dream come true of a whole new world of 'atomically powered peace'. What was presented to them as 'peace' and 'progress' was in fact a catastrophe. As West Europeans and Americans were joyously greeting the first war-free summer in 1946, the nuclear Armageddon in the Marshall Islands was just starting, and it would, like that kiss in OMD's post-apocalyptic song about the Hiroshima bomber called *Enola Gay*, 'never ever fade away'. And how was the sacrifice of these humble people who contributed their 'little all' to the 'progress' of humankind to be remembered? It is sufficient to make a small experiment here: when you see or read the word 'Bikini' today, do you think of the 'hellish roaring blast of ghastly power' that turned the Bikini Atoll into a sinister 'terminal beach', or do you think about a two-piece swimsuit?

Remember the thesis that the Apocalypse is always a 'struggle for meaning'? It is here where this struggle acquires a truly apocalyptic character – namely, it's no coincidence that the history behind the origin of the bathing suit is directly connected to the Bikini Atoll. Not so much to the 'Garden of Eden' full of coconut trees and sandy beaches, but precisely to the 'Terminal Beach'. In July 1946, just a few days after one of the nuclear tests at the Bikini Atoll, the French engineer and designer Louis Réard launched a campaign for his new swimsuit design reasoning that the newspapers were full of news about the nuclear test at Bikini and a swimsuit called 'bikini' could have the same 'atomic' effect.[36] When it hit the French Riviera, it set off an 'explosion' of moral outrage, the Vatican declared it sinful and it was banned in Spain and Italy. But when the legendary fashion editor Diana Vreeland proclaimed that it was 'the most important thing since the atom bomb' (*no kidding!*) and Brigitte Bardot was photographed wearing a bikini on a beach at the Cannes Film Festival, the invention quickly became a commercial success.

And what was the outcome of this 'struggle for meaning'? Even today when we read or hear the word 'bikini' or when we encounter a two-piece swimsuit on the beach, we don't generally think about the nuclear experiments that left levels of radioactivity 1,000 times higher than Chernobyl. Yet, it is the word 'bikini' – like J. L. Borges's 'Aleph' – into which a whole Apocalypse can fit. It is a word through which we can enter the 'doorways into another continuum'. Because it opens an ontological abyss in which it is not only the future of those local populations that disappeared, it is also our own future that is at stake and the future of the planet itself, given that the effects of the nuclear testings won't simply disappear even when the Marshall Islands vanish into the ocean. For instance, Plutonium-239 that was used in these tests has a half-life for radioactive decay of 24,000 years.

So what is finally 'time beyond progress'? It is a time that goes beyond the notion of 'progress' based on a destructive and self-destructive myth that never-ending *expansion*, *extraction* and *exploitation* are leading towards something good for humankind and the planet, when in fact they are leading towards the naked Apocalypse without kingdom, namely to *extinction*. It is precisely 'progress' and its fatal illusion of ever-expanding 'growth' – whether it is the growth of GDP or the growth of nuclear mushrooms and sea levels – that is turning the whole planet into an immense Marshall Islands, a world 'after the Apocalypse'. There is no progress without catastrophe. It is the catastrophe itself that is always already inscribed into progress. As Paul Virilio, the great *dromologue* who died in 2018, famously warned us: 'The shipwreck is consequently the "futurist" invention of the ship, and the air crash the invention of the supersonic airliner, just as Chernobyl meltdown is the invention of the nuclear power station.'[37]

Today we should add: the collision of the nuclear age and climate crisis that is taking the Marshall Islands as one of its first victims is consequently the 'futurist' invention of what we call 'progress'. And the crucial question then becomes, how do we go beyond this fatal concept of 'progress'? If we know that we will never be able to fully prevent the end of the world, for some eschatological threats will always remain out of human control, how do we at least create another end of the world that isn't the nightmare currently unfolding in places where the collision has already begun?

The conclusion is the following: in order to minimize the eschatological tipping points explored in this book, we have to start from the reinvention of time that must be directed against the prevailing ideology and dystopian reality of 'progress'. If the shipwreck was invented simultaneously with the invention of the ship and Hiroshima was invented as soon as the atom bomb was invented, then we have to consider progress as the invention of the catastrophe itself. *Expansion* – whether it is through technological inventions serving further extraction or through the colonization of time by hyper-accelerated global capitalism – *is not progress*. It is leading to *extinction*.

And perhaps no one captured this true meaning of 'progress' as well as Louis-Auguste Blanqui, who wrote *Eternity by the Stars. An Astronomical Hypothesis* (published in 1872) while being held prisoner in the Château du Taureau during the Paris Commune period. In his conclusion of this phantasmagoric manifesto, he writes:

> What we call progress is locked up on each earth and disappears with it. Always and everywhere, on the terrestrial camp, the same drama, the same set, on the same narrow stage, a noisy humanity, infatuated by its own greatness, thinking itself to be the universe and inhabiting its prison like an immensity, only to drown soon along with the globe that has borne the burden of its pride with the deepest scorn. The same monotony, the same immobility in foreign stars. The universe repeats itself endlessly and struts on its legs. Unfazed, eternity plays the same performance in the infinite.[38]

When the clocks are melting in the ontological Garden of Eden, and there is no longer any difference between progress and catastrophe, we might be, indeed, resurrected in Blanqui's 'eternity by the stars', locked up on Earth and disappearing with it. But as the imprisoned revolutionary knew very well, it is only through struggle, even if it means struggle until extinction, that the naked Apocalypse without kingdom can become meaningful, and perhaps, even endurable and joyful. If there is no second coming, no new kingdom, no last judgement coming after the Apocalypse, then we actually have no other alternative but to embrace this eternity by the stars – just like the Blanquian hero of *12 Monkeys* who is caught in a dystopian 'eternal return', but is slowly, as the story unfolds, accepting his fate in a sort of *amor fati*, accepting that there is no escape from one's time. And if there is no escape from our own 'End-Time', if there is nothing but pure nothingness coming after extinction, then we still have the chance – and, indeed, we have the moral duty – to mourn tomorrow's dead today, to struggle not so much for ourselves, but for those to come so that another end of the world could still be possible. So that the 'revelation' might become false.

Postscriptum: 'Revelation' of COVID-19

Penetrating into the live cell of a foreign body, the virus substitutes its own for the cell's substance and transforms it into a factory for the production of new viruses. The changes which it brings about in this way in the life medium of the cell are incomparably deeper and more dramatic than man can ever hope to bring about in his own milieu. The virus is the most perfect being in the cosmos. Its biological organization is nothing less than a machine for producing life in its purest sense.'

Borislav Pekić, *Besnilo* (*Rabies*), 1983

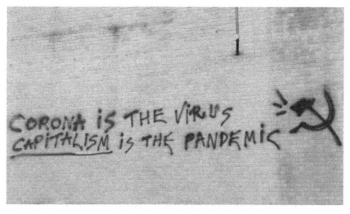

Figure 8: Graffiti on a wall in Toronto, May 2020

From the radiant future that perhaps still seems distant
or 'supraliminal' to all but those who are already struggling to survive the first and immediate effects of the
collison of the nuclear age and climate crisis, we arrive
back to the viral present. Perhaps, this present has
been overwritten by even more cataclysmic events in
the meantime, and we will look towards this moment
with a certain nostalgia, as if we were recalling a time
in which we still had a chance to change our future.
But one thing seems certain even in these times of utter
uncertainty: if there was any recent year that could be
described as the year of the Apocalypse in its original
meaning as 'revelation', then it was 2020. This was a
year when 'the Earth stood still', not because, like in
that good old science fiction movie, an alien came to
warn us that humanity must live in peace, but because
'the most perfect being in the cosmos' – as the great
Serbian writer Borislav Pekić called the virus – arrived.
And as the world was going through a profound change
that affected everything and everyone, everywhere and
in every time, so this 'Apocalypse of COVID-19', understood as 'revelation', served as a unique X-ray machine
that enabled us to understand the architecture of our
world, both as place and time, better than ever before.
The questions that arise in the ruins of our hyper-
accelerated present are the following: are we going to be
able to seize this opportunity 'unveiled' by COVID-19,
this crack in time and space? Will we succeed not just
in mourning tomorrow's dead today but in struggling
for them until extinction? Will we use this chance for a
profound transformation that is needed if we want to
have a future at all?

The reason why this reflection on the COVID-19
pandemic comes at the end of this book lies not only in
the fact that it happened after my visits to the 'future
of places' such as Chernobyl and the Mediterranean,
including a speculative trip to the Marshall Islands.

The current pandemic is undoubtedly an unprecedented historic and planetary event that is nowhere near over as I write this pages; in fact, the WHO has just warned that 'the worst is yet to come'.[1] Nevertheless, the current number of 26 million confirmed COVID-19 cases and 875,000 deaths at the beginning of September 2020, as horrific as they are, will already look quite modest in a few years' time, when catastrophic events (even deadlier viruses), including the nuclear threat and climate crisis, reach the 'eschatological tipping points' and we come even closer to mass extinction. The arguments are as follows: (1) the pandemic, as horrendous as it is right now, is connected to the environmental and climate crisis to the extent that it is about the destructive relation of humans towards nonhuman species and also about the ever-increasing expansion of global capitalism and our encroachment on the planet, including our rapid movement around it (which spreads infections much faster than in any previous historic period); and (2) pandemics of this kind will be part and parcel of much larger catastrophic events that lie ahead.

Just as the WHO was warning that 'the hard reality is this is not even close to being over',[2] a new study published in the scientific journal *PNAS* revealed that researchers in China have discovered a new type of swine flu that is capable of triggering a new pandemic. According to the study, this new virus 'has already acquired increased human infectivity' and 'raises concerns for the possible generation of pandemic viruses'.[3] This all leads to the following question: what if COVID-19 – as dreadful as it already is – is just a small footnote, or rather 'revelation' (Apocalypse in its original meaning), of the things to come? What we have learned in the first half of 2020, as if we were taking part in a collective crash course in pandemics, is that the virus can't be understood as a 'separate' eschatological threat; it is intrinsically connected to global capitalism and climate crisis. To put it simply: the more you destroy nature, the more viruses there will be, and the more likely it is that there will be a domino effect of 'tipping points' leading to total collapse. But the current pandemic is part of a bigger picture, and to the extent that we are all currently obsessed and affected by COVID-19, it is but a footnote to the kind of eschatological event that is yet to come. And this is precisely the reason why the COVID-19 pandemic, this sort of X-ray machine from the future, already carries many important lessons for our struggle for the future.

'Wuhan is everywhere'

There is a saying that I encountered while stuck in quarantine in Vienna during spring 2020, which is being ascribed both to Karl Krauss and Gustav Mahler. It says: 'When the world comes to an end, I'll go to Vienna. There, everything happens 10 years later.' I had already sent a previous version of this book to my patient publisher in late January, when the first news about the appearance of COVID-19 in China reached Vienna. While the much deadlier Black Death – that took around 200 million lives in just four years – needed about ten years to reach Europe from China, COVID-19, thanks to the infrastructure of contemporary global capitalism (flight, trains and other means of transport), needed only a few weeks to become a full-blown pandemic.

Back in early February, as we were watching gigantic Chinese cities being quarantined and resembling a real existing science fiction version of *28 Days Later* and *Blade Runner*, Karl Krauss or Gustav Mahler (whoever was the author of that old saying) already seemed anachronistic. Because what happens in Wuhan obviously doesn't stay in Wuhan. It also happens in Vienna. As

I, together with millions around the world, watched the scenes from the cruise ship *Princess Diamond*, our whole planet – as Slavoj Žižek suggested in one of his early texts on the pandemic – was already turning into a post-apocalyptic cruise ship.[4] Although the privileged passengers of this ship could certainly afford a 'joyful Apocalypse' (*fröhliche Apokalpyse*), just like that Australian couple quarantined on *Princess Diamond* who were photographed ordering wine delivered by a drone,[5] there was no escape from COVID-19.

Then, like earlier pandemics that would often end up with bloody witch-hunts and pogroms, the *virus of racism* started spreading all across the world. In South Korea, more than half a million people petitioned the president to stop Chinese people from entering the country, while Vietnamese shop-owners in Hungary – where Viktor Orbán was blaming migrants, foreign students, opposition politicians and Soros for the spread of the virus – put up signs saying that they are not Chinese.[6] In Italy, the 'ground zero' of Europe's COVID-19 crisis at that time, the leader of the far right Lega Nord party, Matteo Salvini, tweeted critically about the announcement of the first cases of coronavirus in the country. He said: 'And they said we were speculators and alarmists. Open borders, useless people in government. We pray to God that there are no disasters, but whoever has done wrong must pay.'[7] On the same day, the vice-president of the Italian Senate, Ignazio La Russa, recommended using the fascist salute to avoid getting the coronavirus. 'Do not shake hands with anyone, the contagion is lethal. Use the Roman greeting, anti-virus and antimicrobial', he wrote in his official Twitter account.[8]

The *virus of racism* was obviously spreading faster than the virus itself. Around the same time, the Italian economist Tommaso Valletti described an incident on a train in Italy. A teenage Chinese boy boarded the train.

A woman commented loudly: 'There you go, we are all going to be infected.' He replied in perfect Italian with a Roman inflection: 'Ma'am, in my whole life I've seen China only on Google Maps.'[9] A few days later in Ukraine, angry protestors attacked buses carrying people evacuated from the Chinese city of Wuhan. They blocked the roads and began to pelt the buses with stones.[10] At this time, newspapers were still reporting that the bulk of worldwide infected cases of COVID-19 – around 75,000 – were still located in mainland China, where around 2,000 people had died from the virus.[11]

In early March, just a few days before Austria went into full lockdown, articles about China's 'new normal' had already reached Vienna. They were about mass surveillance and public monitoring that were still being referred to as something 'Chinese', as if it wasn't going to happen – in various forms (mainly powered by Silicon Valley companies) – in the West as well. There was an app called Alipay Health Code 'that assigns individuals one of three colour codes based on their travel history, time spent in outbreak hotspots and exposure to potential carriers of the virus'.[12] And as everyone was denouncing China's 'totalitarian measures', the Austrian newspapers were reporting that a new start-up called Swarm Analytics wanted to use geolocation tracking and AI to fight the virus in Tirol, Austria's COVID-19 'ground zero'. A few days earlier, one of Austria's main mobile network operators, A1, had already given the geolocation data of its users to the government, but according to Swarm Analytics this was not enough: AI should control all the public cameras in order to find 'hotspots' where people were gathering and where new restrictions were needed.[13]

Just as I was learning to adapt to the obvious start of the pandemic in Austria, China was already – at least according to newspapers and images we could see on social networks – living the 'new normal', a term that would soon become the leading concept – or more precisely, ideology – of the year 2020. It was a feeling that would recur and perhaps never leave me again, as if a part of the world was already living in the future, while we, in Europe were still in the past. Or were we – at the very same time – someone else's future? What was happening in Vienna after the virus reached Austria, was something that was a near future, with much more dire effects awaiting first the United Kingdom and United States, and then Latin America and Africa.

During one of those early days of COVID-19 in Austria, while I was still in my old apartment closer to Mariahilferstrasse, a whole street was blocked off by the police in the neighbouring Bezirk when suspicion arose that someone in a school with around 500 children was infected with the virus. The test was negative. But fear and paranoia in Vienna were rising. A few days earlier, a train from Italy to Austria was stopped at the border for fear of infection. By then, supermarkets were already noticing higher demand for products such as canned food and pasta. Not only in Austria. One memorable reaction to this phenomenon during those days, which could as well have been a tragicomic sketch from the American sitcom *Seinfeld*, was a video recording of an elderly Italian man filmed at the exit of an empty Italian supermarket emotionally saying: 'The pasta shelves are empty! What's happening? There wasn't this much panic when World War II started!'[14]

And again, what happened in Italy started to happen not only in Austria, but literally all over the world. The respiratory virus was spreading quickly, but so was the *virus of consumerism*. All over the world, where people could afford it, toilet paper suddenly became the most sought-after commodity, and was soon missing from the supermarket shelves. In Germany, the word of the day describing the COVID-19 panic hoarding was '*Hamsterkauf*' ('hamster buying'), while in the United

States there was a joke circulating asking what Trump's legacy would be. Answer: 'He was so full of shit that the country ran out of toilet paper.' When we recall the scenes of empty supermarket shelves in spring 2020 all across the world, couldn't the same be said about global capitalism? Remember the images of empty supermarkets in Venezuela, presented as proof that socialism doesn't work. What about capitalism? Isn't the lack of toilet paper in 2020 all across the world, besides being an interesting psychological and social phenomenon, also a tragicomic reminder that it is precisely capitalism that obviously doesn't work? Not only was there a lack of toilet paper and face masks, but public healthcare systems that had already been destroyed by decades of austerity and privatization were collapsing, people were losing their jobs, while others, who didn't have the luxury to stock up at supermarkets and pretend to be 'hamsters' preparing for the end of the world, were working on the 'frontlines' of the pandemic – from doctors and nurses to truck drivers, supermarket cashiers and workers in Amazon warehouses.

On 13 March, when I was already packed and planning finally to leave Austria, the government announced a 'state of exception', closing everything except supermarkets, pharmacies and gas stations. Sights such as Schönbrunn Palace and St Stephen's Cathedral, museums, theatres, opera houses and many others were closed as well. While the whole western region of Tirol – the popular ski resort where Austria's first cases were reported – was already under total lockdown, the Viennese authorities were transforming the Messehalle Wien, the place of the biggest trade fair in Austria where Conchita Wurst won the Eurovision Song Contest 2015, into a big Lazarett (military-style hospital) for those infected with COVID-19. It looked surreal. As if the 'end of the world' had finally, much sooner than in 10 years, arrived in Vienna. That very same day the WHO announced that Europe had now become the epicentre of the pandemic, with more reported cases and deaths than the rest of the world combined. At that time, more than 132,500 people had been diagnosed with COVID-19 in 123 countries around the world and the total number of deaths had reached around 5,000.[15]

On 16 March 2020, as announced, the 'state of exception' came into effect. And here I was, stuck in Vienna in a friend's apartment[16] in the 5th Bezirk without any chance of returning to Croatia or moving anywhere, a period that would last more than two long months before I was able to exit Austria. We were told only to go out if necessary. All gatherings of more than five people were banned. Then very soon only members of a family or household could be together in public spaces. The Austrian Chancellor Sebastian Kurz said that 'freedom of movement in our country is going to be massively limited', adding that these measures were 'necessary to defend the health of the Austrian people'.[17] For the first time, as a foreign citizen who came to Vienna as a 'guest worker' (*Gastarbeiter*) at the Burgtheater, planning to leave in mid-March but stuck due to the pandemic until late May, I asked myself the question: what about us, foreigners stuck in a city where the 'end of the world' was supposed to arrive 10 years later, will our health also be 'defended'? The Austrian Chancellor is telling us to have social contact only with the people with whom we live, saying it is 'the most difficult situation we've ever faced in the post-war years'.[18] Who are the 'we'? Is it just the Austrians? We, whoever we are, should leave our house (do we have a house?) only for work (do we have a job?) that could not be postponed, to buy necessary food (do we have the money?) and to help others (can we even help ourselves?). In the following days, I would notice police cars driving around Vienna with open windows and loud music playing a popular Austropop song called 'I am from Austria'. As I would find out later from the newspaper, they had official instructions from the authorities to do this in order to raise the morale of those who are obviously 'from Austria'. And, again, the same question returned: what about us – EU citizens – who are not from Austria but happen to be stranded here in the midst of a pandemic? What about all those who are not EU citizens and who don't have any rights in this country, no health insurance and no ability to return to their own countries? And, on a more general level, what about the millions of refuges who are struggling to survive in packed camps or trying to reach Europe via dangerous routes only to be pushed back by Frontex and border police, without any luxury of 'self-isolation' or 'social-distancing'? Are they also part of that 'we', and couldn't we say that they are facing the most difficult situation in the post-war years every single day?

Around the time that Austria closed its borders with Germany, Hungary and Slovenia, so Germany closed its borders with France, Switzerland, Austria, Denmark and Luxembourg. The Czech Republic and Slovakia banned all foreigners from entering their countries, except those with a residence permit. On 17 March, with so many lockdowns already in full swing all over Europe, an unprecedented event took place: the European Union closed all its external borders. In a twist of irony, exactly 30 years earlier, in 1990, the winning song of the Eurovision Song Contest in Zagreb – then still Yugoslavia – was 'Insieme: 1992' by Toto Cutogno from Italy. It was a song about unity (*'insieme'* meaning 'together') and a world without borders, with the memorable lyrics 'Unite, unite, Europe'. This Europe now seemed so far away, as if it was from another world. The already existing division between the centre and the periphery of the European Union was deepening even further, with wealthier countries protecting themselves first (for instance, by rejecting the 'mutualization' of debt or banning the export of medical protection gear including masks, gloves and protective suits), before thinking about 'unity'. In some corners of Europe, both south and north, like in Serbia or France, political leaders – both Aleksandar Vučić and Emmanuel Macron – were talking about an 'invisible enemy' and the army was sent onto the streets of both Belgrade and Paris. What was already becoming clear – as a sort of political 'revelation' – was how different European countries adopted sometimes similar and sometimes radically different strategies for dealing with this 'invisible enemy'. The COVID-19 Apocalypse was an X-ray machine that revealed everything that was rotten both with global capitalism and with our governments, both with the so-called 'free market' and with the 'nation-state' (with a few exceptions such as New Zealand and Iceland).

Even if some people – from the former White House chief strategist Steve Bannon to Ukrainian politician Andriy Shevchenko – were comparing COVID-19 to the nuclear disaster in Chernobyl, the virus was not the same as radioactivity. However, what brings them together is not only the corruption of different states and the 'cover-ups' or the downplaying of a serious global threat, but the very invisibility of the danger. The virus is an eschatological threat that is so uncanny and terrifying precisely because you can't see it. But what we can see (and could have seen in the weeks following the outbreak) once the virus has done its job are the military trucks carrying the coffins of hundreds of dead bodies. Yesterday in Iran, today in Italy, tomorrow in the United States and Brazil.

To paraphrase Günther Anders again, today we should perhaps say: 'Wuhan is everywhere'. This doesn't imply that the same scale of quarantine or number of deaths as in Wuhan occurred 'everywhere'; it means that the age of pandemic trespasses across borders, nation-states and national identities. The virus simply doesn't care if you call it 'Chinese' or an 'invisible enemy'. You can even send the army and shut down borders, but the 'the most perfect being in the cosmos' will always find its way. When the world is going to end, you can go to Vienna, but to expect it to arrive 10 years later now looks like an utterly romantic hope from the last century. And just as the nuclear age and climate crisis know no borders, so the age of the pandemic, which might have only just started, also happens everywhere.

Eschatological tipping points

Even if Wuhan was 'everywhere', it was not everywhere at the same time. During the peak of the COVID-19 pandemic in Europe, it often felt as if, from the perspective of China, we were in the past, while in the eyes of other parts of the world – those where the pandemic would hit really hard in the coming months – our present could have been interpreted as the future. As Austria was already in full lockdown, with me in 'self-isolation' in Vienna, I would hear from my friends in Berlin and Zagreb that even at this moment people were still partying, even having 'illegal apartment parties'. When, for instance, on 22 March, the UK's prime minister Boris Johnson, after preaching about 'herd immunity', finally announced the closing of pubs, restaurants, gyms and clubs, we in Vienna had already been living under such measures for over a week.

Around the same time, we could have seen surreal images from the United States, with beaches full of people as if it were – as Alex Shephard wrote in his article 'The pandemic movie of our time isn't *Contagion*' – a scene from Steven Spielberg's *Jaws*.[19]

In a manner similar to that adopted by Donald Trump with regard to the COVID-19 pandemic, the fictional Mayor Vaughn sees the shark as a hoax: 'It's all psychological. You yell "Baracuda", everybody says, "Huh? What?" You yell "Shark", we've got a panic on our hands on the Fourth of July.' The reason why Spielberg's mayor doesn't close the town is summer dollars. On another occasion, he says to a reporter in a truly Trumpian way: 'As you can see, it's a beautiful day. The beaches are open and people are having a wonderful time.' But then, on 4 July, the shark kills a child. And something similar happened thanks to the dangerous child who was President of the United States during the COVID-19 pandemic. He was also claiming that people were having a wonderful time, while in fact the shark of COVID-19 was already swallowing up the United States.

While Austria and many other countries in Europe were under lockdown with heavy restrictions of movement (in some countries, like France, Italy, Spain, Macedonia, Bosnia and Serbia, even curfew), the famous Bondi Beach in Australia was full of people as if it was New Year's Day. Some even suggested it should be renamed 'Corona Beach'. Unlike the mayor in *Jaws*, one of Australia's mayors advised people to stay at home, but many were simply ignoring 'social distancing'. And it's certainly not the first time in history that some parts of the world were already living through 'apocalyptic realism' (the spread of a contagious virus, empty streets, closed theatres, restriction of movement and even curfew), while elsewhere people were partying as if there were no tomorrow.

Just before the outbreak of the First World War, Stefan Zweig recalls – in his autobiographic masterpiece *The World of Yesterday* (sent to his publisher the day before he committed suicide with his second wife in 1942) – something that could easily be a description of our contemporary 'heterochronicity',[20] different times that are simultaneously present as sorts of 'other places' (*heterotopias*) that are always, even if unbeknownst to its 'inhabitants', interacting. It was summer 1914, a summer that was '*sommerlicher*' ('more summerish') than any summer before. The famous Austrian writer was holidaying in Baden, near Vienna, a small romantic city that was once Beethoven's favourite *Sommeraufenthalt*, describing it as follows:

> In light summer dresses, gay and carefree, the crowds moved about to the music in the park. The day was mild; a cloudless sky lay over the broad chestnut trees; it was a day made to be happy in. The vacation days would soon set in for the adults and children, and on this holiday they anticipated the entire summer, with its fresh air, its lush green, and the forgetting of all daily cares.[21]

They didn't yet know that the war had started – with Gavrilo Princip assassinating the Archduke Franz Ferdinand in Sarajevo – in an 'other place' and 'other time' that would soon become their time and would take place throughout the whole world. One century later, not unlike the privileged 'carefree' Austrians who were enjoying the cloudless sky and forgetting their daily cares as the war started, many people were enjoying the days that were 'made to be happy in' on Bondi Beach or in clubs, at illegal parties, post-apocalyptic bunkers and various other *heterotopias*, even as the virus was rapidly spreading all over the place.

An even more sinister depiction of heterochronicity was described by Zweig in a short article that appeared in 1918 under the title 'A carefree life', the year of the Spanish flu. It's a story about a visit to the 'care-free people' (*Sorglosen*) in the Alps of St Moritz. The *Sorglosen* live a luxurious life in the fresh air; they laugh and ski, play polo and hockey. They dance. They are masked. And, as if he was writing about our current times, Zweig notes: '

> Europe falls into rubble. The gypsy band fiddles away. Ten thousand people die every day. Dinner is over and the masked ball begins. Widows sit shivering in all the chambers of the world. A bare-shouldered marquise steps forward, a masked Chinese opposite. Masks and more masks pour in. And truly, they are real – not a human face amongst them. The mirror sconces are lit. The dance commences: sweet, soft rhythms, while elsewhere ships sink into the deep and trenches are stormed.[22]

In a similar manner, in March 2020, while tens of thousands of people were being infected by COVID-19 every day and the number of deaths in Italy exceeded that registered in China, beaches in some corners of the world were still full of people. At the same time, some people were already living through various eschatological threats that were very often simultaneously present. As the medievalist Bruce M. S. Campbell has shown in his book *The Great Transition: Climate, Disease and Society in the Late-Medieval World*, in the 1340s, multiple eschatological threats – war, more adverse climate, and finally the Black Death – were also present at the same time, until they were combined in what Campbell calls a 'perfect storm'.[23] COVID-19 was certainly not the Black Death, but it was indeed a similar 'perfect storm' – or, following Thesis 6 from the Introduction to this book, an 'eschatological tipping point' – that hit the world in 2020.

It had already been a week of lockdown in Austria. After moving to a new apartment and unable to return to Croatia, I was slowly adapting to the 'new normal' that was best described, a few months later, by Naomi

Klein as the 'Screen New Deal'.[24] It was the time when the EU was warning that the continent's broadband networks might crash as millions – undoubtedly the highest number in human history – were working from home or watching Netflix, YouTube or pornography, gaming or just chatting about the Apocalypse. Then, on the morning of 22 March, I woke up and switched on my phone only to find messages from my sister who was in Zagreb 'self-isolating' for a week after returning on the last flight from Munich. The first thing I saw were photographs of her partner carrying their 4-year-old child on his shoulders and walking through the main street of Ilica, which was full of debris. I'm quickly becoming aware this was not another COVID-19-related nightmare, but reality. Then I read the message feed:

Earthquake
5.3
Everything was shaking
It's like war
They told us not to go home

I hadn't read any news. I had just woken up and expected the 'regular' COVID-19 reality of 'self-isolation' in Vienna. Little did I understand that another eschatological threat had just become real in an 'other place', a place of my family and friends. And even if I was in another place, suddenly the 'other time', their time, became my time as well. I immediately called my sister and she described what had happened. A powerful earthquake – the strongest since 1880 – hit the capital of Croatia around 6:30 a.m. She and her partner immediately took their child, my 4-year-old nephew, and escaped from the fifth floor of their shaking building, rushing to the closest empty park. Many other people gathered, most of them without masks, but still at a distance of a few metres. Then they somehow reached the house of my parents in another part of the city. They were fine. But my sister's 'self-isolation' was now over, exacerbating another eschatological threat besides the earthquake, namely the possibility that our 71-year-old father, already with a heart issue and diabetes, and a heavy smoker, might become the quintessential victim of COVID-19. My sister later told me that everyone was shocked, except him. Even during the time of the war in the 1990s, when Yugoslavia was collapsing, he would never run to the basement from the third floor of our building when air-raid sirens went off.

Now, instead of a brutal war, two eschatological threats combined – a pandemic and an earthquake. An official message from Croatia's government captured this contradictory threat in the best possible manner: 'We request citizens to leave their homes because of the earthquake, but to respect the coronavirus measures at the same time and keep social distance.' While I was still sleeping in Vienna, the citizens of Zagreb – including my beloved ones – have been awoken by two such contradictory eschatological threats: if you want to stay safe you should stay at home; if you want to stay safe you should immediately leave your home. After the earthquake hit, as if it was an old Hollywood disaster movie, around 1,500 people escaped Zagreb by car and drove towards the south, to the coast of Croatia. Among them, 40 were supposed to be 'self-isolating'. Everyone was scared about what this would mean for the spread of the contagion in a country that was (and luckily would be) handling the pandemic surprisingly well. And once again, we could see how people react in 'other times' and 'other places' – some enact beautiful acts of solidarity, while others go into full Darwin mode and only care about their own future. As Michel Foucault stated in his fourth principle of his *Of Other Places*, 'the heterotopia begins to function at full capacity when men arrive at a sort of absolute break with their traditional time'.[25] And this was precisely what happened in Zagreb – but also all across the world (faced with different eschatological threats combined with climate crisis, the nuclear age and the COVID-19 pandemic). It was a break with traditional time.

The responses on a common mailing group of my friends in Zagreb who started a chat in those times of self-isolation, sharing experiences and mostly dark humour, offers a beautiful and surreal glimpse into the heterochronicity of 'other places', places where people were awoken both by a quite unexpected earthquake and by a pandemic – two eschatological threats at the same time:

> Ivo: 'We watched Variola Vera [an old Yugoslav film about the outbreak of smallpox in Yugoslavia in 1972], I dreamt that I was dying of variola. Next scene: everything is shaking...'

> Sara: 'Luka and me were watching Ocean 13 to relax a bit, that movie in which they stimulate an earthquake to fuck up a casino. And here we are, they fucked us. Comrades, I am looking forward to the New Year when we will all hug again.'

> Cane: 'My father was in the toilet when it started. Did anyone have similar luck?'

> Poga: 'Luckily the earthquake hit during the times of quarantine, otherwise it would hit someone at a party who would be buried at the dance floor. Like that alien from "I will survive", who is in the end hit by a disco ball.'

> Tina: 'We are ok, moved with cats to Vodovodna, my apartment is pretty ruined and we don't know when we can get back.'

Tena: 'They advise not to drink water from the pipeline
for some time. I don't know whether this is checked
information, but rather buy bottled water today.'

I immediately called my sister. She told me the water, indeed, has a strange taste. But how could she go to buy bottled water if she was supposed to be in 'self-isolation'? Everything is confusing. Even the Croatian prime minister is saying that Croatia is confronted by 'two contradictory threats'. The one is the virus that forces you to stay at home, the other is the earthquake that forces you to leave it. My sister can't return to the previous apartment as it is damaged by the earthquake. So she and her child went to my parents' house, opening again the fear that our father might get infected by the virus. But at least on the ground floor they are safer from the earthquake than on the fifth floor.

The most shocking images from Zagreb came from the hospitals: there was a photograph of a group of mothers dressed in nightgowns hugging their newborn babies in a parking lot as they were evacuated from a damaged maternity hospital in freezing temperatures. They had to get out to protect themselves and their children. But being outside was dangerous not only because of COVID-19, but also because it had just started to snow, as if the whole situation wasn't already surreal enough. Then there were images of women and incubators being moved to a new location with the help of the army. And also, one of the two spires of Zagreb's iconic cathedral – with a cross on it – had collapsed. Coronavirus, snow in spring, a series of earthquakes, a cross collapsing, what is next? That's how many inhabitants in Zagreb, and those of us worried in 'other places' such as Vienna, felt during that March in 2020. Already by the next day, since humour is perhaps the best way to deal with the Apocalypse, a group of citizens had organized, and thousands joined in, an online event called 'Waiting for Godzilla in Zagreb at 06:30'.[26] Dress code: pyjamas.

On the one side dark humour, on the other the feeling of utter helplessness, especially if you are stuck in an 'other place', a *heterotopia* that was not of your own choosing. All I can do is to call my family and friends, and when not doing that, I can just scroll through the news and images from Zagreb, catapulting myself into an even deeper feeling of helplessness. I'm in self-isolation, already not able to move, and all I can do in a situation in which my natural tendency would be to immediately jump out of the apartment and help my loved ones, is to worry, make phone calls, search the news and worry even more after every image I see or story I hear. A dear friend lost her apartment. Another is in hospital. There was another earthquake just now. The pandemic is still here. The head is exploding. Or rather, it is imploding. All this is just too 'supraliminal' (Thesis 7). Then, on that very same day, comes news from another surreal *heterotopia*: Angela Merkel is going into quarantine after meeting a doctor who tested positive for coronavirus. I, obviously being in an 'other time' and 'other place', sent a message to my sister: 'Angela Merkel is in quarantine.' She immediately responds, bringing me back to her time and place: 'I couldn't care less about Merkel at this moment.'

Only a week later, in the 'Exclusion Zone' of Chernobyl, in another dystopian example of 'eschatological tipping points' – as if the COVID-19 pandemic was not enough – the biggest wildfires ever seen in that region started.[27] They were 'ignited' by climate crisis – hot, dry and windy weather that is becoming more common in Ukraine. An estimated 57,000 hectares around Chernobyl had already burned by then, which is around 22 per cent of the total area of the 'Exclusion Zone'.[28] In mid-April, plumes of smoke caused smog in Kyiv, 110 kilometres away, and higher levels of radioactivity than usual were detected. And just like in 1986, the smoke and ash crossed borders. The Norwegian Radiation and Nuclear Safety Authority registered a small increase of caesium-137 concentrations in the air in Norway.[29] Besides caesium-137, the 'Exclusion Zone' is heavily contaminated with strontium-90, americium-241, plutonium-238 and plutoniom-239. Plutonium particles are the most toxic ones: they are estimated to be around 250 times more harmful than caesium-137. Fires that are now happening every year in Ukraine, Belarus, and Russia, where 5 million people still live in contaminated areas, release these toxic particles into the air and wind transports them over long distances, making the threat of radioactivity present again.[30]

The catastrophe of Chernobyl, explored in the second chapter of this book, is obviously still present. And it is never going to disappear. On the contrary, the greater the climate crisis (hotter summers, dry weather and stronger winds), the more radiation will return to the environment (through the air, clouds and oceans). Add to this a pandemic and you will come to the perfect embodiment of the world 'after the Apocalypse'. As the 'Exclusion Zone' was burning in one place and Merkel was in quarantine in an 'other place', Zagreb was still shaking. And it wouldn't stop shaking. According to the Croatian Seismologic Service, after two powerful earthquakes of 5.5, and 4.8 on the Richter scale that hit Zagreb on 22 March, Zagreb would be hit by almost 1,000 earthquakes – with a magnitude higher than 0.6 on the Richter scale – in only 24 days.[31] When I told this to my friend from Guatemala who was stuck in 'self-isolation' in Berlin at that moment, she responded: 'Get used to it, it's like that all the time in Guatemala.'[32] Then, in a beautiful gesture of transnational solidarity, she gave me practical advice for my family and friends in Zagreb, very simple but original ideas of how to be better prepared for the future – 1,000 earthquakes.

The revolution of breathing

'It's like that all the time here', could have been something a person of colour said to a privileged white person complaining about the virus of police brutality and structural injustice. On 25 May 2020, at the peak of the COVID-19 pandemic that was reaching 100,000 deaths in the United States alone by that time, Minneapolis police officers arrested George Floyd, a 46-year-old African American man, after he was accused of buying cigarettes with a counterfeit $20 bill. Just 17 minutes after the first police car had arrived at the scene, he was dead, with his neck beneath the knee of a police officer, while two other officers were making sure he couldn't move. For nearly nine minutes he was gasping for air and repeatedly groaning, 'please, I can't breathe'.

Before being killed by the police, Floyd had suffered the same fate as millions of – especially black – Americans during the coronavirus pandemic: he had lost his job as a bouncer at a restaurant when Minnesota's governor issued a stay-at-home order. He had five children. But he wasn't killed by COVID-19, he was killed by the virus of police brutality and of a system that generates inequality depending on race and class. Black people are nearly three times more likely than whites to be killed by the police, and, as we would soon find out, the COVID-19 mortality rate for black Americans was also three times the rate for white Americans.[33] The autopsy on George Floyd's corpse showed that, before he lost his job due to COVID-19 and before he was killed by the police, he was indeed infected with the virus.[34]

This is not the first time that a black man couldn't breathe because a police officer was choking him to death. The exact same words 'I can't breathe' were repeated 11 times by Eric Garner, another black man who was put in a deathly chokehold by the police in New York in 2014, after he was accused of selling loose cigarettes on the street. Garner later died at a hospital and a grand jury declined to indict the police officer, sparking nationwide Black Lives Matter (BLM) demonstrations. In his book *Breathing: Chaos and Poetry*, published just a year before the brutal murder of George Floyd and the COVID-19 pandemic, the Italian philosopher Franco 'Bifo' Berardi claims these words express the general sentiment of our times: 'Physical and psychological breathlessness everywhere, in the megacities choked by pollution, in the precarious social condition of the majority of exploited workers, in the pervading fear of violence, war, and aggression.'[35] It is precisely *respiration* that, according to Bifo, can help us to understand the contemporary chaos: the process of 'breathing with chaos' or 'chaosmosis', which he defines as 'osmosis with chaos', is where a 'new harmony emerges, a new sympathy, a new syntony'.[36]

Our contemporary difficulty in breathing is both literal and allegorical. It is the result of a short circuit of an era that, at the same time, combines the precariousness of life produced by global capitalism and the complexity linked to the pandemic of a respiratory virus that acts as what Bifo calls a 're-coder' of our lives. A year before hundreds of thousands would die because of a new respiratory virus and just a year before George Floyd was choked to death, Bifo, who himself lives with asthma, claimed that we need a 'sense of asthmatic solidarity'. The murder of George Floyd was a brutal repetition of the death of Eric Garner. No wonder Garner's mother said that watching how George Floyd pleads 'I can't breathe' before dying was like having a 'déjà vu all over again'.[37] But this time the injustice that happened in one corner of the world led to a global movement of solidarity against the structural injustice and racism that black people encounter every day.

Many people in the world are scared of COVID-19, but many of them are more scared of being suffocated to death by the police. Millions of unemployed workers are also scared of COVID-19, but many of them are more worried about how to survive until the next month. Even before the outbreak of the pandemic, the *Gilets Jaunes* (Yellow vests movement) argued that, while some are concerned about the 'end of the world', they were worried about 'the end of the month'. And they couldn't be more right. While the techno-utopians, our postmodern version of 'futurists', were imagining a future on Mars or (in the less utopian case) in their private post-apocalyptic bunkers, inventing Cybertrucks and Cyberhouses, the working class that was already broken by decades of austerity measures and precarity was hardly surviving the 'end of the day'.

The 'Revelation of COVID-19' was thus not just a revelation of multiple eschatological threats that are simultaneously interlinked or inducing each other (climate crisis was not only exacerbating the threat of a virus, but was at the same time triggering the threat of radioactivity), it was also a lesson that every Apocalypse is always already political. If all the current events, 'years and years' that have become '100 seconds to midnight', teach us anything, it is the important lesson that there is a clear connection between our current political system and the end of the world, between the way we manage our global economy and the way we will vanish from the devastated face of the Earth. The COVID-19 pandemic left hundreds of millions of workers unemployed, not to mention the effects on the informal sector that accounts for more 60 per cent of the global workforce (around 2 billion people).[38] And everywhere it hit, it 'unveiled' – in the sense of the original meaning of the Greek *apokalýp(tein)* – the fundamental inequalities and class divisions inscribed into our societies and produced by the global capitalist system.

Since the oubtreak of the COVID-19 pandemic, we have heard it said so many times that the 'virus doesn't discriminate', while in fact everywhere it is clear that it is the system itself that discriminates. If you were already poor or vulnerable, one of the 'essential workers' or among many without a house or any possibility of 'self-isolation' and 'social distance', the chances of being infected were higher. While immunology has become a class question, we have also witnessed a weaponization of the class struggle. Already in April 2020, the United Nations warned of 'biblical' famine due to COVID-19.[39] Even before the pandemic, 821 million people went to bed hungry every night all over the world, the causes of which are a combination of wars, natural disasters and economic crises in countries such as Yemen, Syria, Sudan, Lebanon, Congo and Ethiopia.[40] With the locust swarms that hit Africa in spring 2020 and the outbreak of COVID-19, the UN warned that we are facing 'the worst humanitarian crisis since World War II'.[41] According to an analysis by the World Food Program released on 21 April 2020, COVID-19 puts 265 million at risk of a 'hunger pandemic' by the end of the year.[42] In this sense, COVID-19 was a 'revelation' of not only a broken system, but a system that was built that way, through centuries of colonialism and expansion of capitalism. And as the pandemic was, in different rhythms, coming closer to all places in the world, we could have witnessed a sort of 'hunger games' already. The rich and upper class who were usually living in cities immediately fled to the outskirts or to the countryside; the middle class was confined to apartments and was suddenly immersed in the 'Screen New Deal' or a sort of COVID-1984; while the working class – frontline workers, the unemployed and informal sector, the global poor living in slums or refugees in camps – had neither the choice nor the luxury of 'self-isolation' and 'social distancing'. It was the system itself that was isolating and distancing them from the rest of society.

After the murder of George Floyd, it seemed that a global movement was connecting the various hetero-chronicities and heterotopias together, and very soon we could have seen not only a rage against the virus of racism but also a rage against global capitalism and colonialism. It started with protesters kneeling on the neck of the toppled statue of the notorious slave trader Edward Colston for eight minutes (the length of time that George Floyd had spent gasping for air), before toppling him into Bristol's harbour. Then other colonial monuments faced a similar fate: they were decapitated or demolished, inspiring a wave of similar actions across the world tearing down butcherers such as Christopher Columbus, whose 'discovery' led to the extinction of indigenous communities across the Americas, and King Leopold II, who killed as many as 10 million Africans during the period of his brutal regime in Congo. The 'revelation' of these symbolic acts that were, by throwing the monuments into the dustbin of history, rewriting it, was the following: in order to create the possibility of futurability that would be based on justice and final decolonization of the whole planet (the decolonization from capital itself), we need transnational cooperation and solidarity in the sense of going beyond borders and nation-states, radical spatial and political inventions that could not only minimize the existing eschatological threats, but also succeed in creating a different end of the world. And, at the same time, we need a temporal shift that would, by going beyond generations and times, include a radical commitment to the future, even if – or precisely because – this future, at some point, means extinction. One of the first revolutionaries who explicitly talked about *extinction* was Blanqui, who in his *Instructions for an Armed Uprising* in 1868 simply says: 'The duty of a revolutionary is always to struggle, to struggle no matter what, to struggle to extinction.'

Today, thanks to the 'Revelation of COVID-19' even those who were not yet radicalized and would usually treat terms such as 'struggle to extinction' as an overstatement by a crazy old French revolutionary, became revolutionaries themselves. It was the situation itself that radicalized them. In a powerful open letter 'I want my death to make you angry', Emily Pierskalla, a nurse fighting the local outbreak of COVID-19 in Minnesota, gave the best example of this political subjectivation. She was outraged with Donald Trump's administration's response to the pandemic, emotionally overwhelmed with the scenes of suffering she witnessed and in fear of her own life. Emily wrote:

> *If I die, I don't want to be remembered as a hero.*
> *I want my death to make you angry too.*
> *I want you to politicize my death.*
> *I want you to use it as fuel to demand change in this industry, to demand protection, living wages, and safe working conditions for nurses and ALL workers.*
> *Use my death to mobilize others.*
> *Use my name at the bargaining table.*
> *Use my name to shame those who have profited or failed to act, leaving us to clean up the mess.*[43]

Only a few weeks later, George Floyd was murdered, and the words of a nurse from Minnesota were becoming true. Hundreds of thousands all across the world who joined the Black Lives Matter protests were using the name of George Floyd and shaming those who had profited or failed to act, those who were using even more police violence as a response to a brutal murder by the police. It was not just a protest against a case of injustice in Minnesota, it was rage against the militarization of our societies, both inside and outside, within our societies and between our societies divided by walls, biopolitics and epidemiological neoliberalism. As we all know by now, when our faces are covered by protective masks, it is hard to breathe, it is hard to be heard. Yet, when global capitalism merged with authoritarianism and fascism is working actively to make voices that call for a radical change silent, from the black people and indigenous communities to the 'essential workers' and high-tech whistleblowers like Chelsea Manning and Edward Snowden, or courageous publishers like Julian Assange, it is precisely the face mask that is no longer just a symbol of our times of planetary suffocation (be it because of police brutality, air pollution, wildfires or a respiratory virus), but may just as well be the symbol of resistance.

The fossilized status quo obviously lacks the imaginative and moral means to take a (r)evolutionary leap into a future worth living, because its imagination and interests are based only on extraction, exploitation and further expansion. Instead of breathing, it is a system that is generating suffocation. This is how from the eschatological threats explored in this book – from the nuclear threat to climate change – we arrive at the need for system change. This was the 'Revelation of COVID-19'. And if we want to construct a future beyond the current real existing dystopia, we should be pledging our allegiance to the planet itself and its future, a sort of planetary allegiance that would go beyond mere cosmopolitanism. Instead of just being 'citizens of the world', which is usually reserved only for humans, this planetary ethics would need to treat other species and the planet itself as 'commons'. And in order to survive and preserve both the biosphere and the semiosphere, we need to understand time itself as a sort of 'planetary commons', whether it is the past in the sense of human history and evolution or the future in the sense of the time that remains both for us and other species. When the post-apocalyptic fiction section has been moved to current affairs, our only alternative is simple: mass extinction or a radical reinvention of the world after the Apocalypse.

Another end of the world is still possible.

Soundtrack

Bonnie 'Prince' Billy – 'I See A Darkness'
Still Corners – 'Sad Movies'
Šo Mazgoon – 'Zatočen'
Damir Imamović – 'O bosanske gore snježne'
Chromatics – 'Tick of the Clock'
Sigur Rós – Untitled 3 (Samskeyti)
Ember – *Seven Samurai*
Orchestral Manoeuvres in the Dark – 'Enola Gay'
Robert Wyatt – 'Foreign Accents'
Primal Scream – 'Swastika Eyes'
Godspeed You Black Emperor – 'East Hastings'
Tindersticks – 'See My Girls'
Sarathy Korwar – 'Bol' (feat. Zia Ahmed & Aditya Prakash)
Kraftwerk – 'Radioactivity'
LVMEN – 'No. 1'
EmperorX – 'Don't Change Color, Kitty'
Barnbrack – 'The Unicorn'
Q Lazzarus – 'Goodbye Horses'
Low – 'Lullaby'

Notes

Introduction

1 'China expands coronavirus outbreak lockdown to 56 million people', Al Jazeera, 25 January 2020. https://www.aljazeera.com/news/2020/01/china-expands-coro navirus-outbreak-lockdown-fast-tracks-hospital-200124 201635848.html.

2 'Wuhan lockdown "unprecedented", shows commitment to contain virus: WHO representative in China', Reuters, 23 January 2020. https://www.reuters.com/article/us-chi na-health-who-idUSKBN1ZM1G9.

3 'Coronavirus spurs to China to suspend tours abroad and Xi to warn of a 'grave situation', *New York Times*, 25 January 2020. https://www.nytimes.com/2020/01/25/ world/asia/china-coronavirus.html.

4 See, for instance, Paul Mason, 'We must be told what Cummings and Palantir are doing with NHS data', open Democracy, 4 June 2020. https://www.opendemocracy.net/ en/opendemocracyuk/we-must-be-told-what-cummings-and-palantir-are-doing-nhs-data/.

5 Naomi Klein, 'Screen New Deal', The Intercept, 8 May 2020. https://theintercept.com/2020/05/08/andrew-cuomo-eric-schmidt-coronavirus-tech-shock-doctrine/.

6 Ibid.

7 'Coronavirus: which governments are bailing out big polluters?', *Climate Change News*, 20 April 2020.

https://www.climatechangenews.com/2020/04/20/coronavirus-governments-bail-airlines-oil-gas/.

8 See the American science fiction film *The Day the Earth Stood Still* (1951), directed by Robert Wise, about an alien who neutralizes electricity on the whole planet, in order to force humans to live in peace.

9 Déborah Danowski and Eduardo Viveiros de Castro, *The Ends of the World*. Polity, 2017.

10 The reception of Günther Anders is finally changing, mainly thanks to the work of the Austrian philosopher Konrad Paul Liessmann and the French philosopher Jean-Pierre Dupuy, including many other scholars and institutions such as the Günther Anders Archive in Vienna, and the International Günther Anders Society also based in Vienna: https://www.guenther-anders-gesellschaft.org.

11 Günther Anders, 'Apocalypse without kingdom', e-flux, February 2019. https://www.e-flux.com/journal/97/251199/apocalypse-without-kingdom/.

12 Felix Guattari, 'Integrated world capitalism and molecular revolution', text presented at the Conference on Information and/as New Spaces of Liberty (CINEL), which took place in Rio de Janeiro in 1981. English translation available here: https://adamkingsmith.files.wordpress.com/2016/10/integrated-world-capitalism-and-molecular-revolution.pdf (italic SH).

13 Ibid.

14 415 ppm CO_2 refers to the record level of carbon dioxide in our atmosphere reached in May 2019, the first time this has happened in human history. https://www.sciencealert.com/it-s-official-atmospheric-co2-just-exceeded-415-ppm-for-first-time-in-human-history.

15 'More than 90% of glacier volume in the Alps could be lost by 2100', European Geosciences Union, press release, 9 April 2019. https://www.egu.eu/news/482/more-than-90-of-glacier-volume-in-the-alps-could-be-lost-by-2100/.

16 Total number of glaciers in the Alps according to the European Geosciences Union. For reference see previous footnote.

17 'UK climate activists hold "funeral procession" for the planet', Al Jazeera, 12 October 2019. https://www.

aljazeera.com/news/2019/10/uk-climate-activists-hold-funeral-procession-planet-191012183408672.html.

18 Sami Khatib, 'Brushing Walter Benjamin's "Angel of History" against the grain', *Crisis & Critique*, vol. 3. no. 2, 2016, p. 38.

19 Manjana Milkoreit et al., 'Definining tipping points for social-ecological systems scholarship: an interdisciplinary literature review', *Environmental Research Letters*, vol. 13, no. 3, 2018. https://iopscience.iop.org/article/10.1088/1748-9326/aaaa75.

20 'Climate crisis: 11,000 scientists warn of "untold suffering"', *Guardian*, 5 November 2019. https://www.theguardian.com/environment/2019/nov/05/climate-crisis-11000-scientists-warn-of-untold-suffering.

21 Günther Anders. *Die Antiquiertheit des Menschen 1. Über die Seele im Zeitalter der zweiten industriellen Revolution*. Beck, 2002(1956), pp. 262–263; and 'Wenn ich verzweifelt bin, was geht's mich an? Gespräch mit Günther Anders', in Mathias Greffrath, ed., *Die Zerstörung einer Zukunft. Gespräche mit emigrierten Sozialwissenschaftlern*. Rowohlt, 1979, pp. 19–57.

22 https://thebulletin.org/doomsday-clock/current-time/#.

23 Ibid.

24 'These charts show how coronavirus has "quieted" the world', *National Geographic*, 8 April 2020. https://www.nationalgeographic.com/science/2020/04/coronavirus-is-quieting-the-world-seismic-data-shows/.

25 Günther Anders, 'Apocalypse without kingdom'. https://www.e-flux.com/journal/97/251199/apocalypse-without-kingdom/.

26 Paul Tilich, *The Protestant Era*. University of Chicago Press, 1948, p. 155.

27 'The life of Günther Anders (1902–1992)', Internationale Günther Anders Gesellschaft. https://www.guenther-anders-gesellschaft.org/vita-english.

28 Pablo Servigne, Raphaël Stevens and Gauthier Chapelle, *Another End of the World Is Possible. Living the Collapse (and Not Merely Surviving It)*, trans. Geoffrey Samuel. Polity, 2020.

29 Ibid.

30 See: Jean-Pierre Dupuy, *The Mark of the Sacred*. Stanford University Press, 2013.

31 Joanna Zylinska, *The End of Man: A Feminist Counterapocalypse*. University of Minnesota Press, 2018.

Chapter 1   Back to the Future Mediterranean

1 'President Gravybrain says a bunch of truly bizarre shit about windmills and the universe', *Qizmodo*, 23 December 2019. https://earther.gizmodo.com/president-gravybrain-says-a-bunch-of-truly-bizarre-shit-1840607633.

2 Ibid.

3 The farthest inhabited island off the Croatian mainland. For more on Vis, see Srećko Horvat, *Poetry from the Future*. Penguin, 2019.

4 The ferry is named after the Renaissance poet and writer Petar Hektorović (1487–1572) from the island of Hvar.

5 Lyall Watson, 'A brief eerie history of how the wind makes us crazy', *Literary Hub*, 13 August 2019. https://lithub.com/a-brief-eerie-history-of-how-the-wind-makes-us-crazy/.

6 Ibid.

7 Ibid.

8 Herodotus, *The Persian Wars*, trans. A. D. Godley, 1920, Book IV, 173. https://en.wikisource.org/wiki/Herodotus_The_Persian_Wars_(Godley)/Book_IV. (Thanks to Pawel Wargan)

9 See Fernand Braudel, *Memory and the Mediterranean*. Vintage Books, 2002; and Predrag Matvejević, *Mediterranean: A Cultural Landscape*. University of California Press, 1999.

10 For more about the geology of the Komiža bay, see: https://geopark-vis.com/en/geology/geotrails/geotrail-komiza.

11 Glenn Albrecht, '"Solastalgia": a new concept in health and identity', *PAN: Philosophy, Activism, Nature*, 2005, pp. 44–59.

12 Ibid., p. 49.

13 Glenn Albrecht et al., 'Solastalgia: the distress caused by environmental change', *Australasian Psychiatry*, 2007.

14 Timothy A. C. Gordon et al., 'Grieving environmental scientists need support', *Science*, 11 October 2019. https://science.sciencemag.org/content/366/6462/193.1.

15 Ibid.
16 '"They should be allowed to cry": ecological disaster taking toll on scientists' mental health', *Independent*, 10 October 2019. https://www.independent.co.uk/environment/ecolo gical-disaster-mental-health-awareness-day-scientists-climate-change-grief-a9150266.html.
17 Ibid.
18 See Jean-Pierre Dupuy, *A Short Treatise on the Metaphysics of Tsunamis*, trans. M. B. DeBevoise. Michigan State University Press, 2015.
19 Quoted from ibid., p. 2.
20 'New elevation data triple estimates of global vulnerability to sea-level rise and coastal flooding', *Nature Communications*, 29 October 2019. https://www.nature.com/articles/s41467-019-12808-z.
21 Ibid.
22 'Up to 630 million people could be threatened by rising seas', *New Scientist*, 29 October 2019. https://www.newscientist.com/article/2221273-up-to-630-million-people-could-be-threatened-by-rising-seas/.
23 Tim Woollings, 'A battle for the jet stream is raging above our heads', *The Conversation*, 14 November 2019. https://theconversation.com/a-battle-for-the-jet-stream-is-raging-above-our-heads-125906.
24 Lana Reimann et al., 'Mediterranean UNESCO World Heritage at risk from coastal flooding and erosion due to sea-level rise', *Nature Communications*, 16 October 2018. https://www.nature.com/articles/s41467-018-06645-9.
25 'The ocean is teeming with microplastics – a million times more than we thought, suggests new research', World Economic Forum, 13 December 2019. https://www.weforum.org/agenda/2019/12/microplastics-ocean-plastic-pollution-research-salps/.
26 Ibid.
27 'Human consumption of microplastics', *Environmental Science and Technology*, vol. 53, no. 122, 5 June 2019, pp. 7068–7074.
28 'World faces "climate apartheid" risk, 120 more million in poverty: UN expert', United Nations, 25 June 2019. https://news.un.org/en/story/2019/06/1041261.

29 Ibid.
30 'Record-breaking wave in Adriatic Sea', WeatherZone, 14 November 2019. https://www.weatherzone.com.au/news/record-breaking-wave-in-adriatic-sea/530516.
31 'Venice closes St Mark's Square as floods hit for third time in week', *Guardian*, 17 November 2019. https://www.theguardian.com/world/2019/nov/17/venice-closes-st-marks-square-as-high-water-threatens-again.
32 'Italian council is flooded immediately after rejecting measures on climate change', CNN, 15 November 2019. https://edition.cnn.com/2019/11/14/europe/veneto-council-climate-change-floods-trnd-intl-scli/index.html.
33 'The future of Venice and its lagoon in context of global change', UNESCO, 2011. http://www.unesco.org/new/fileadmin/MULTIMEDIA/FIELD/Venice/pdf/rapporto1_very%20high%20res.pdf.
34 'Venice still waiting for Moses to hold back the seas', Reuters, 13 November 2019. https://www.reuters.com/article/us-italy-weather-venice-mose/venice-still-waiting-for-moses-to-hold-back-the-seas-idUSKBN1XN2EQ.
35 'Can I still visit Venice after the worst floods in 50 years?', *Telegraph*, 15 November 2019. https://www.telegraph.co.uk/travel/destinations/europe/italy/veneto/articles/can-i-visit-venice-floods-severe-weather-warning/.
36 Ibid.
37 'Travel advice: is Venice safe?' *The Sun*, 14 November 2019. https://www.thesun.co.uk/travel/10336593/safe-travel-venice-holiday-floods/.
38 Ibid.
39 'Despite catastrophic flooding, much of Venice's art appears safe for the moment', Artnet, 14 November 2019. https://news.artnet.com/art-world/despite-flooding-venice-art-safe-1704279.
40 'Ibiza of the Alps under scrutiny as emails tell new virus tale', *Bloomberg*, 9 May 2020. https://www.bloomberg.com/news/articles/2020-05-09/ibiza-of-the-alps-under-scrutiny-as-emails-tell-new-virus-tale.
41 Thomas Mann, *Death in Venice*, trans. Martin C. Doege from the 1912 edition. https://archive.org/stream/DeathInVenice/DeathInVenice-ThomasMann_djvu.txt.

42 'Venice floods threaten priceless artwork and history', *Washington Post*, 17 November 2019. https://www.washingtonpost.com/history/2019/11/17/venice-floods-threaten-priceless-artwork-history-unique-way-life/.

43 'Boats pass over where our land was: Bangladesh's climate refugees', 4 January 2018. https://www.theguardian.com/global-development/2018/jan/04/bangladesh-climate-refugees-john-vidal-photo-essay.

44 'Fire at Notre-Dame Cathedral leads to expressions of heartbreak across the world', *New York Times*, 15 April 2019. https://www.nytimes.com/2019/04/15/world/europe/paris-cathedral-fire.html.

45 Ibid.

46 Neil Smith, 'There's no such thing as a natural disaster', 11 June 2016. https://items.ssrc.org/understanding-katrina/theres-no-such-thing-as-a-natural-disaster/.

47 Ibid.

48 Seen from a point of view of world-system theory (for instance, Immanuel Wallerstein, *The Modern World-System*. Vol. I: *Capitalist Agriculture and the Origins of the European World-Economy in the Sixteenth Century*), influenced by Fernand Braudel's notion of *le long* seizième siècle (1450–1640), the so-called 'long sixteenth century' may be taken for the starting point of a global society and world economy.

49 See Jason W. Moore, 'The Capitalocene. Part I: On the nature and origins of our ecological crisis', *Journal of Peasant Studies*, 2017.

50 Félix Guattari, *The Three Ecologies*. Athlone Press, 2000, p. 52.

51 Ibid.

52 For the definition of 'living currency', see the first English translation of the seminal work by Pierre Klossowski, *Living Currency*. Bloomsbury, 2017.

53 Carlo Maria Martini and Umberto Eco, *Belief or Nonbelief? A Confrontation*. Arcade, 2000.

54 'Venice flooding: what does the extreme weather mean for tourists?', *Independent*, 13 November 2019. https://www.independent.co.uk/travel/news-and-advice/

venice-flooding-latest-weather-rain-water-italy-travel-tourists-a9201501.html.

55 'Flooding in Venice and the "apocalypse" of St Mark's', *Corriere Della Sera*, 14 November 2019. https://www.corriere.it/international/19_novembre_14/flooding-venice-and-the-apocalypse-of-st-mark-s-4aef2d88-0713-11ea-8c46-e24c6a436654.shtml.

56 Ibid.

Chapter 2 'Enjoy Chernobyl, Die Later'

1 Quote from: https://www.youtube.com/watch?v=9n977DCuNF0.

2 Ibid.

3 Some of these images are based on a good collection of German TV news available on the following YouTube link. https://www.youtube.com/watch?v=9n977DCuNF0.

4 'Strahlende Wildschweine im deutschen Wald', *Deutschlandfunk Kultur*, 25 April 2019. https://www.deutschlandfunkkultur.de/33-jahre-nach-tschernobyl-strahlende-wildschweine-im.1001.de.html?dram:article_id=447114.

5 International Physicians for the Prevention of Nuclear War (IPPNW). https://www.ippnw.org/milestones.html.

6 Katrin Jordan, '"Die Wolke, die an der Grenze haltmachte", Der Reaktorunfall von Tschernobyl 1986 im französischen Fernsehen,' *Themenportal Europäische Geschichte*, 2014. https://www.europa.clio-online.de/essay/id/fdae-1633.

7 Günther Anders, 'Ten theses on Chernobyl', Libcom. https://libcom.org/library/ten-theses-chernobyl---günther-anders#footnoteref5_bgfga4l.

8 Ibid.

9 'Über die Bombe und die Wurzeln unserer Apokalypse-Blindheit,' in *Die Antiquiertheit des Menschen*, vol. 1. Beck, 1956.

10 Günther Anders, Commandments in the atomic age', in Claude Eatherly and Günther Anders, *Burning Conscience*. Monthly Review Press, 1961. https://aphelis.net/wp-content/uploads/2013/04/ANDERS_1957_Commandments_in_The_Atomic_Age.pdf.

11 Ibid., p. 13.

12 Günther Anders, 'Ten Theses on Chernobyl'. https://libcom.org/library/ten-theses-chernobyl---günther-anders#footnoteref5_bgfga4l.

13 Svetlana Alexievich, *Chernobyl Prayer*, trans. Anna Gunin and Arch Tait. Penguin, 2013, p. 24.

14 Kate Brown, *Manual for Survival: A Chernobyl Guide to the Future*. Norton, 2019.

15 Anders, *Commandments in the Atomic Age*, in Eatherly and Anders, *Burning Conscience*.

16 Hannah Arendt, *The Human Condition*. University of Chicago Press, 1958, p. 3

17 See Günther Anders, 'Das Prometheische Gefälle', in *Die Antiquiertheit*, vol. 1, pp. 17–18. *Die Antiquiertheit des Menschen. Band II: Über die Zerstörung des Lebens im Zeitalter der dritten industriellen Revolution*, C. H. Beck, 1956.

18 Günther Anders, *Tagesnotizen. Aufzeichnungen 1941–1979*. Suhrkamp Verlag, 2006, pp. 24–25. (Trans. Srećko Horvat.)

19 Ibid, p. 27.

20 Ibid.

21 Ibid., pp. 111–112.

22 Ibid., p. 119.

23 Albert Speer, *Inside the Third Reich*, trans. Richard and Clara Winston. Macmillan, 1970, p. 56.

24 Anders, *Tagesnotizen*, pp. 55–56.

25 Ibid, p. 141.

26 Ibid, p. 162.

27 Ibid, p. 145.

28 See W. Benjamin and A. Lacis, 'Naples', in Walter Benjamin, *Reflections: Essays, Aphorisms, Autobiographical Writings*. Shocken, 1986.

29 Meilee D. Bridges, 'Necromantic pathos in Bulwer-Lytton', in Lorna Hardwick and James I. Porter (eds), *Pompeii in the Public Imagination from Its Rediscovery to Today*. Oxford University Press, 2011, p. 94.

30 See Sigmund Freud, *Delusion and Dream in Jensen's Gradiva*, 1907.

31 'Can a restored Pompeii be saved from 'clambering' tourists?', *New York Times*, 25 October 2019. https://

www.nytimes.com/2019/10/25/travel/pompeii-resto
ration-overtourism.html.

32 'Chernobyl: now opens to tourists', *Guardian*, 13 December
2010. https://www.theguardian.com/world/2010/dec/13/
chernobyl-now-open-to-tourists.

33 'Chernobyl to become official tourist attraction, Ukraine
says', CNN, 11 July 2019. https://edition.cnn.com/travel/
article/chernobyl-tourist-attraction-intl-scli/index.html.

34 Ibid.

35 Svetlana Alexievich, *Voices from Chernobyl: The Oral
History of a Nuclear Disaster*, trans. Keith Gessen. Picador,
2006. https://archive.org/stream/VoicesFromChernobyl-
TheOralHistoryOfANuclearDisaster/VoicesFromCher
nobyl-TheOralHistoryOfANuclearDisasterBySvetlanaAl
exievich_djvu.txt.

36 'Radioactive ice-cream and penis graffiti: how toxic TV
tourists took over Chernobyl', *Guardian*, 20 December
2019. https://www.theguardian.com/tv-and-radio/2019/
dec/20/radioactive-ice-cream-and-penis-graffiti-how-
toxic-tv-tourists-took-over-chernobyl.

37 State Agency of Ukraine on Exclusion Zone Management.
https://ukraine-kiev-tour.com/2019/chernobyl-tours-
statistics.html.

38 'Best post-Apocalypse whiskey: new limited edition
Walking Dead bourbon', *Forbes*, 1 August 2019.
https://www.forbes.com/sites/larryolmsted/2019/08/01/
best-post-apocalypse-whiskey-new-limited-edition-
walking-dead-bourbon/#291efe294a82.

39 'Scientists produce "Atomik" vodka from Cherobyl
grain', *Guardian*, 8 August 2019. https://www.
theguardian.com/environment/2019/aug/08/
scientists-produce-atomik-vodka-from-chernobyl-grain.

40 'In Germany, fears of food contamination', 19 April 2006.
https://www.spiegel.de/international/spiegel/looking-
back-at-chernobyl-in-germany-fears-of-food-contami
nation-a-411272.html.

41 'Tinder wants users to find love in the Apocalypse',
WIRED, 24 September 2019. https://www.wired.com/
story/tinder-swipe-night-wants-users-to-find-love-in-the-
apocalypse/.

42 'Tinder's video game will show you how prospective matches handle an apocalypse', 12 October 2019. https://www.dailydot.com/debug/tinder-swipe-night/.

43 See Roland Barthes' text 'Toys', in *Mythologies*, Editions du Seuil, 1957.

44 'Fashionable face masks: "Trying to make something horrific seem appealing"', *Guardian*, 13 January 2020. https://www.theguardian.com/fashion/2020/jan/13/fashionable-face-masks-trying-to-make-something-horrific-seem-appealing.

45 Ibid.

46 'As air pollution gets worse, a dystopian accessory is born', *Vox*, 19 March 2019. https://www.vox.com/the-goods/2019/3/19/18262556/face-mask-air-filter-pollution-vogmask-airpop.

47 'Fashionable face masks'.

48 Michel de Montaigne, *Shakespeare's Montaigne: The Florio Translation of the Essays, A Selection*, NYRB, 2014, p. 24.

49 Svetlana Boym, *Another Freedom: The Alternative History of an Idea*, University of Chicago Press, 2012, p. 250.

50 Umberto Eco, *Travels in Hyperreality: Essays*, trans. William Weaver. Harcourt, Brace & Company, 1986, pp. 7–8.

51 'Trump administration wants to reclassify leaking nuclear waste to avoid cleaning it up, say officials', *Independent*, 9 January 2019. https://www.independent.co.uk/news/world/americas/nuclear-waste-trump-radioactive-washington-state-hanford-atomic-bombs-a8719021.html.

52 'Trump suggests "nuking hurricanes" to stop them hitting America', *Guardian*, 26 August 2019. https://www.theguardian.com/us-news/2019/aug/26/donald-trump-suggests-nuking-hurricanes-to-stop-them-hitting-america-report.

53 'US security officials "considered return to nuclear testing" after 28-year hiatus', Guardian, 23 May 2020. https://www.theguardian.com/world/2020/may/23/us-security-officials-considered-return-to-nuclear-testing-after-28-year-hiatus.

54 'Chernobyl's Reactor Four control room opens to tourists', *Independent*, 2 October 2019. https://www.independent.

co.uk/travel/news-and-advice/chernobyl-reactor-four-open-tourists-ukraine-nuclear-disaster-a9129591.html.

55 Alexievich, *Voices from Chernobyl*.

56 'Chernobyl's literary legacy, 30 years later', *The Atlantic*, 26 April 2016. https://www.theatlantic.com/entertainment/archive/2016/04/chernobyls-literary-legacy/479769/.

Chapter 3 Marshall Islands Are Everywhere

1 'Key missile defense installation will be uninhabitable in less than 20 years', *Scentific American*, 1 March 2018. https://www.scientificamerican.com/article/key-missile-defense-installation-will-be-uninhabitable-in-less-than-20-years/.

2 Greg Dvorak, "The Martial Islands': making Marshallese masculinities between American and Japanese militarism', *The Contemporary Pacific*, 'Re-membering Oceanic Masculinities', vol. 20, no. 1, 2008, p. 55.

3 'Seafloor scar of bikini a-bomb test still visible', BBC, 10 December 2019. https://www.bbc.com/news/science-environment-50724632.

4 'A ground zero forgotten', *Washington Post*, 27 November 2015. https://www.washingtonpost.com/sf/national/2015/11/27/a-ground-zero-forgotten/.

5 'Operation Castle', Nuclear weapon archive. http://nuclearweaponarchive.org/Usa/Tests/Castle.html.

6 'What is the difference between a hydrogen bomb and an atomic bomb?', *Time*, 22 September 2017. https://time.com/4954082/hydrogen-bomb-atomic-bomb/.

7 'Background gamma radiation and soil activity measurements in the northern Marshall Islands', *PNAS*, 15 July 2019. https://www.pnas.org/content/116/31/15425.

8 'A poison in our island', ABC, 3 May 2019. https://www.abc.net.au/news/2017-11-27/the-dome-runit-island-nuclear-test-leaking-due-to-climate-change/9161442?nw=0.

9 'Key missile defense installation will be uninhabitable in less than 20 years'.

10 'SpaceX private rocket shifts to island launch', *SPACE*, 12 August 2005. https://www.space.com/1422-spacex-private-rocket-shifts-island-launch.html

11 Ibid.

12 'Huge waves and disease turn Marshall Islands into "a war zone", health official says', *Los Angeles Times*, 5 December 2019. https://www.latimes.com/environ ment/story/2019-12-05/marshall-islands-waves-flood ing-disease-war-zone.

13 'World leaders urged not to COP out of climate action in Madrid', *RNZ*, 3 December 2019. https://www.rnz.co.nz/international/pacific-news/404689/world-leaders-urged-not-to-cop-out-of-climate-action-in-madrid.

14 'Marshall islanders: migration patterns and health-care challenges', *Migration Policy*, 22 May 2014. https://www. migrationpolicy.org/article/marshall-islanders-migration-patterns-and-health-care-challenges.

15 'A poison in our island'.

16 Frank Kermode, *The Sense of an Ending. Studies in the Theory of Fiction* Oxford University Press, 2000 (1967), p. 95.

17 Déborah Danowski and Eduardo Viveiros de Castro, *The Ends of The World*. Polity, 2016, p 104

18 Ibid., p. 15

19 'Ocean warming is speeding up, with devastating conse-quences, study shows', Inside Climate News, 14 January 2020. https://insideclimatenews.org/news/14012020/ocea n-heat-2019-warmest-year-argo-hurricanes-corals-marine-animals-heatwaves.

20 Günther Anders, *Wir Eichmannsöhne: offener Brief an Klaus Eichmann*, Beck, 2002, p. 56.

21 Günther Anders, 'Theses for the Atomic Age', *The Massachusetss Review*, vol. 3, no. 3, Spring, 1962, p. 493.

22 Günther Anders, 'Ten Theses on Chernobyl'. https://libcom.org/library/ten-theses-chernobyl---günther-anders#footnoteref5_bgfga4l.

23 Ibid.

24 Zeitschrift für Semiotik: 'Und in alle Ewigkeit: Kommmunikation über 10,000 Jahre: Wie sagen wir unsern Kindeskindern wo der Atommüll liegt?', 3/6, 1984: https://www.semiotik.tu-berlin.de/menue/zeitschrift_fuer_semi otik/zs_hefte/bd_6_hft_3/#c185967.

25 Zoosemiotics: study of the use of signs among animals,

biosemiotics, study of the production and interpretation of signs in the biological realm.

26 Thomas Sebeok, 'Communication measures to bridge ten millennia', April, 1984, prepared by Research Center for Language and Semiotic Studies, Indiana University, for Office of Nuclear Waste Isolation, Battelle Memorial Institute, Columbus, OH. Full report: https://www.osti. gov/servlets/purl/6705990.

27 Philipp Sonntag, 'Künstlicher Mond am Himmel und Datenbank im Keller'. https://www.semiotik.tu-berlin.de/ menue/zeitschrift_fuer_semiotik/zs-hefte/bd_6_hft_3/.

28 Françoise Bastide und Paolo Fabbri, 'Lebende Detektoren und komplementäre Zeichen: Katzen, Augen und Sirenen'. https://www.semiotik.tu-berlin.de/menue/zeitschrift_fuer _semiotik/zs_hefte/bd_6_hft_3/#c185968.

29 'Reducing the likelihood of future human activities that could affect geologic high-level waste repositories', *Technical Report*, May 1984. https://www.osti.gov/biblio/ 6799619.

30 Sandia Report, 'Expert judgment on markers to deter inadvertent human intrusion into the Waste Isolation Pilot Plant', 1993. https://prod-ng.sandia.gov/techlib-noauth/access-control.cgi/1992/921382.pdf.

31 Tim Maly, 'A message to the future', *Works That Work*, No. 3. https://worksthatwork.com/3/message-to-the-future/share/ e8758f8c69f28bb2a0a1ff8d8a91196e.

32 'Nuclear waste: keep out for 100,000 years', *Financial Times*, 14 July 2016. https://www.ft.com/content/db87c16c-4947-11e6-b387-64ab0a67014c.

33 Günther Anders, 'Apocalypse without kingdom', February 2019. https://www.e-flux.com/journal/97/251199/apocaly pse-without-kingdom/.

34 This and the following quotes come from J. G. Ballard, 'The Terminal Beach'. https://biblioklept.org/2015/06/01/ read-j-g-ballards-story-the-terminal-beach/.

35 'Bikini – the Atom island' (1946), Periscope Film LLC archive. Full movie available here: https://www.youtube. com/watch?v=zri2knpOSqo.

36 Patrik Alac, *The Bikini: A Cultural History*. Parkstone Press, 2002.

37 Paul Virilio, *The Original Accident*. Polity, 2007, p. 5. (dromologue = analyst of the phenomena of acceleration)
38 Louis-Auguste Blanqui, *Eternity by the Stars. An Astronomical Hypothesis*. Contra Mundum Press, 2013, p. 149.

Postscriptum: 'Revelation' of COVID-19
1 'Coronavirus: worst could be yet to come, WHO warns', BBC, 29 June 2020, link: https://www.bbc.com/news/world-53227219.
2 Ibid.
3 Honglei Sun, Yihong Xiao, et al., 'Prevalent Eurasian avian-like H1N1 swine influenza virus with 2009 pandemic viral genes facilitating human infection', *PNAS*, 29 June 2020. https://www.pnas.org/content/early/2020/06/23/1921186117
4 Slavoj Žižek, 'We are all in the same boat now – and it's the *Diamond Princess*', Die Welt, 6 February 2020. https://www.welt.de/kultur/kino/article205828983/Slavoj-Zizek-We-re-all-in-the-same-Boat-now-und-it-s-the-Diamond-Princess.html.
5 'Ausie couple ordered wine via drone on quarantined coronavirus cruise ship', *The Australian*, 13 February 20202. https://www.theaustralian.com.au/world/aussie-couple-ordered-wine-via-drone-on-quarantined-corona-virus-cruise-ship/news-story/516f46032a3ce626bc51e0cdfdf12585.
6 'Why don't you stay home? Coronavirus sparks racism fears', *Financial Times*, 1 February 2020. https://www.ft.com/content/eeda65ea-4424-11ea-a43a-c4b328d9061c.
7 Ibid.
8 Ibid.
9 Tommaso Valletti on Twitter, 1 February 2020. https://twitter.com/tomvalletti/status/1223572925342797824?lang=en.
10 'Coronavirus: Ukrainian protesters attack buses carrying China evacuees as panic over outbreak spreads', *Independent*, 21 February 2020. https://www.independent.co.uk/news/world/europe/coronavirus-ukraine-evacuee-protesters-attack-buses-china-zelensky-a9348896.html.

11 Ibid.

12 '"The new normal": China's excessive coronavirus public monitoring could be here to stay', *Guardian*, 9 March 2020. https://www.theguardian.com/world/2020/mar/09/the-new-normal-chinas-excessive-coronavirus-public-monitoring-could-be-here-to-stay.

13 'Swarm Analytics will mit AI-Verkehrskameras im Kampf gegen das Coronavirus helfen', *Trending Topics*, 18 March 2020. https://www.trendingtopics.at/swarm-analytics-will-mit-ai-verkehrskameras-im-kampf-gegen-das-coronavirus-helfen/.

14 '"The pasta shelves are empty": Italy continues to grapple with COVID-19', *Euronews*, 28 February 2020. https://www.youtube.com/watch?v=C2nAL01xOpw.

15 'Coronavirus: Europe now epicentre of the pandemic, says WHO', BBC, 13 March 2020. https://www.bbc.com/news/world-europe-51876784.

16 Thank you, Sabina Sabolović.

17 'Coronavirus: people in Austria told to only go out if necessary', *The Local*, 15 March 2020. https://www.thelocal.at/20200315/austria-bans-gatherings-of-more-than-five-people-over-coronavirus.

18 Ibid.

19 Alex Shephard, 'The pandemic movie of our time isn't *Contagion*. It's *Jaws*', *The New Republic*, 20 March 2020. https://newrepublic.com/article/156991/pandemic-movie-time-isnt-contagion-its-jaws.

20 A term borrowed from biological language used by Michel Foucault in his lecture '*Des spaces autres*' (1967). English translation available here: https://web.mit.edu/allanmc/www/foucault1.pdf.

21 Stefan Zweig, *The World of Yesterday*, University of Nebraska Press, 1964, pp. 214–215.

22 Stefan Zweig, 'Bei den Sorglosen', in *Die schlaflose Welt* ('The Sleepless World'), *Essays 1909–1941*, 4th edn. Fischer Verlag, 2003, pp. 110–111. I owe this reference to the writer and former director of Stefan Zweig Zentrum – Klemens Renoldner.

23 Bruce M. S. Campbell, *The Great Transition: Climate,*

Disease and Society in the Late Medieval World. Cambridge University Press, 2016.

24 Naomi Klein, 'Screen New Deal', *The Intercept*, 8 May 2020. https://theintercept.com/2020/05/08/andrew-cuomo-eric-schmidt-coronavirus-tech-shock-doctrine/.

25 Michel Foucault, 'Of other spaces: utopias and heterotopias', originally published in French, 1967. Available in English here: https://web.mit.edu/allanmc/www/foucault1.pdf.

26 'Doček Godzile u utorak, 24.3, u 6:30 u Zagrebu', Monitor.hr, 23.3. https://www.monitor.hr/godzila/.

27 'Chernobyl still burns', Greenpeace, 23 April 2020. https://www.greenpeace.org/international/story/30198/chernobyl-still-burns-forest-fires-ukraine-nuclear-radiation/.

28 Ibid.

29 https://www.dsa.no/nyheter/95164/svaert-lave-nivaaer-av-radioaktivt-cesium-maalt-i-finnmark.

30 'Chernobyl still burns'.

31 'Pogledajte kako je Zagreb pogodilo gotovo tisuću potresa u 24 dana', *Tportal*, 18 April 2020. https://vijesti.hrt.hr/605834/pogledajte-kako-je-zagreb-pogodilo-995-potresa-u-24-dana.

32 Thank you, Renata Avila.

33 'Black Americans dying of Covid-19 at three times the rate of white people', *Guardian*, 20 May 2020. https://www.theguardian.com/world/2020/may/20/black-americans-death-rate-covid-19-coronavirus.

34 'George Floyd was infected with COVID-19, autopsy reveals', *Reuters*, 4 June 2020. https://uk.reuters.com/article/uk-minneapolis-police-autopsy/george-floyd-was-infected-with-covid-19-autopsy-reveals-idUKKBN-23B1JH.

35 F. B. Bifo, *Breathing: Chaos and Poetry*, Semiotext(e). MIT Press, 2019, p. 15.

36 Ibid, p. 31.

37 'Eric Garner's mother says ...', *Insider*, 27 May 2020. https://www.insider.com/george-floyd-death-eric-garner-mother-i-cant-breathe-2020-5.

38 'More than 60 per cent of the world's employed population are in the informal economy', International Labour Organization (ILO), 30 April 2018. https://www.ilo.org/ global/about-the-ilo/newsroom/news/WCMS_627189/ lang--en/index.htm.

39 'UN warns of 'biblical' famine due to Covid-19 pandemic', France24, 22 April 2020. https://www.france24.com/ en/20200422-un-says-food-shortages-due-to-covid-19-pandemic-could-lead-to-humanitarian-catastrophe.

40 Ibid.

41 Ibid.

42 World Food Programme. https://www.wfp.org/news/ covid-19-will-double-number-people-facing-food-crises-unless-swift-action-taken.

43 Emily Pierskalla, 'I want my death to make you angry'. https://mnnurses.org/want-my-death-make-you-angry/? fbclid=IwAR1RtfnuDzMhnqUUu1P0qXq2y_imoXi9w tbxdLIeEaUgAQ1qNbc4WdP8swM.